5 -
D

"Stephen Cloobeck's book covers the life of a modern-day business genius. I've known him for decades, and he has never changed. He is cocky, self-assured, aggressive, arrogant, self-confident, and always focused. He's not afraid to confront anyone (including me) when he feels it's appropriate. But when all the brashness passes, and it does quickly, one sees a person with a social conscience, a person who is known for his generosity. Stephen Cloobeck is a good person, a creator of thousands of jobs, an innovator, and to many, a friend."

—Former US Senator *Harry Reid*

"Stephen J. Cloobeck is the best in the business. He told me so himself."

—*Dr. Frank Luntz,* political consultant, pollster, and communications expert

"Stephen Cloobeck's story shows that anything is possible when good leaders don't just fight but strategically collaborate for deserving causes. It merits being told, studied, and, hopefully, replicated."

—*Roger Dow,* president and CEO of the U.S. Travel Association

"Whether you're a business leader or emerging entrepreneur, there's a lot of wisdom from Stephen Cloobeck about how to be successful."

—*Robert Shapiro,* internationally renowned litigator and serial business entrepreneur

"I've learned invaluable business lessons from Stephen—most importantly, his unwavering belief in the Meaning of Yes. He created a groundbreaking and innovative 24/7 service culture that always places guests first. People across the globe are changed by these core values every day."

—*Mike Flaskey,* current CEO of Diamond Resorts International

*SASHA — CHECK'N — ALWAYS CHECK'N,*

STEPHEN J. CLOOBECK

# CHECKING IN

## Hospitality-Driven Thinking, Business, and You

Foreword by Mike Milken

GREENLEAF
BOOK GROUP PRESS

This publication is designed to provide accurate and authoritative information in regard to the subject matter covered. It is sold with the understanding that the publisher and author are not engaged in rendering legal, accounting, or other professional services. If legal advice or other expert assistance is required, the services of a competent professional should be sought.

Published by Greenleaf Book Group Press
Austin, Texas
www.gbgpress.com

Distributed by Greenleaf Book Group

For ordering information or special discounts for bulk purchases, please contact Greenleaf Book Group at PO Box 91869, Austin, TX 78709, 512.891.6100.

Design and composition by Greenleaf Book Group
Cover design by Greenleaf Book Group

Publisher's Cataloging-in-Publication data is available.

Print ISBN: 978-1-62634-552-2

eBook ISBN: 978-1-62634-553-9

Audiobook: 978-1-62634-554-6

Part of the Tree Neutral® program, which offsets the number of trees consumed in the production and printing of this book by taking proactive steps, such as planting trees in direct proportion to the number of trees used: www.treeneutral.com

Printed in the United States of America on acid-free paper

18 19 20 21 22 23   10 9 8 7 6 5 4 3 2 1

First Edition

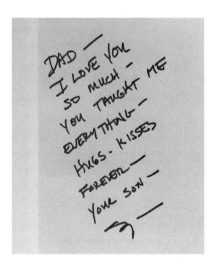

*To my father, my best friend and hero. RIP.*

# CONTENTS

Yes!

When we interact with service providers, that's the only response we ever want to hear.

*Yes*, I can take care of that for you. *Yes*, I understand. *Yes*, I'll do all I can. *Yes*, your request is my top priority.

Hospitality, at its core, is about relationships, and every employee at every company has the ability to utter those responses.

But as anyone who's ever checked into a hotel, called a customer service line, or eaten in a restaurant knows—they often don't. Why?

In the pages that follow, my longtime friend Stephen Cloobeck lays out his vision for how he's helped empower his employees around the world to value the meaning of "yes."

This book is a reminder that the simplest lessons can be the most easily overlooked and that a return to fundamentals is often necessary to turn around a struggling business. These lessons apply far beyond the hospitality sector, too. Stephen captures it well when he describes an expensive consultant's report written about a flailing company he had just acquired: "It was full of numbers, figures, and charts . . . [but] where were the sections on our people, our talent?"

I had the great fortune of counting the late Nobel economist Gary Becker among my friends. I first read his seminal work when I was at Berkeley in the mid-1960s. The father of human capital theory, as he was known, shaped my thinking about what really makes a company great. It's not brand, or technology, or product. It's the leadership and the people who work for the company.

As a financier, I focused first on a company's leadership. Whether it was Ted Turner at CNN, or Steve Ross at Time-Warner, or John Malone at Liberty, we sought visionaries who stood for something bigger than making a profit, who were great communicators, and who truly cared for their employees in a way that made their employees care about the company.

Great leaders have the ability—to paraphrase Marcel Proust—to see the world through new eyes. They can communicate with and appreciate the experiences of employees, customers, and other stakeholders, and adjust accordingly. They exhibit empathy and apply it to improving the organization.

The idea of a "great company" is a bit of a misnomer, then. There are great leaders who assemble great teams and instill a drive to accomplish great things together. When that happens, people call the result a "great company."

Two examples come to mind.

Akio Morita was only twenty-five years old when he began his nearly five-decade run as the head of Sony. The company produced Japan's first transistor radio in 1955, then followed up with a pocket-sized version two years later. The fact that the product didn't *actually* fit in a pocket was not an issue: Morita provided his sales team with custom shirts with larger pockets. Not a believer in market research, Morita later wrote that "our plan is to lead the public with new products rather than ask them what kind of products they want."

When Morita's health failed and he stepped down in 1994, the company was on top of the world with a diversified portfolio that included film studios (Columbia Pictures, Tristar), a record company (Sony Music Entertainment), and a lineup of iconic consumer electronic products, including the Walkman, the Handycam, the Trinitron, and the Discman, to name a few.

By 1997, Sony was a $34 billion company. That's the year Steve Jobs returned to lead Apple, which was then worth about $1.65 billion. It took twenty-one Apples to make one Sony.

Jobs drove tremendous growth at Apple through the 2000s until his passing in 2011, at which time *his* company boasted the iconic devices: the iPod, the Mac, the iPhone, and iPad. (Two other interesting parallels between the two men: Jobs billed the iPod as "1,000 songs in your pocket," and he believed "people don't know what they want until you show it to them.")

As of the time of this writing, in March 2018, Apple is the most valuable company in the world with a $913 billion market cap, while Sony is at $65 billion. Today, it takes fourteen Sonys to make one Apple. In just over two decades, the two companies experienced a relative change in value of nearly three hundred times.

### Apple vs. Sony — 1997 Market Value
(21 Apples = 1 Sony)

Billion

| | |
|---|---|
| $40 | |
| $30 | $34.3 Billion |
| $20 | |
| $10 | |
| $0 | $1.65 Billion |
| | Apple    Sony |

### Apple vs. Sony — 2018 Market Value
(14 Sonys = 1 Apple)

Billions

| | |
|---|---|
| $900 | $913 Billion |
| $800 | |
| $700 | |
| $600 | |
| $500 | |
| $400 | |
| $300 | |
| $200 | |
| $100 | $65 Billion |
| $0 | |
| | Apple    Sony |

Jobs understood that leadership and human capital are the key drivers of success: "Innovation has nothing to do with how many R&D dollars you have. When Apple came up with the Mac, IBM was spending at least one hundred times more on R&D. It's about the people you have [and] how you're led."

Morita and Jobs didn't set out to sell widgets and gadgets. They sought to improve lives. They were going to change the world . . . and they did. Early in the pages that follow, Stephen makes an intriguing point along these lines: The world's five largest companies today, all of which are what most would consider *technology* companies, don't define themselves that way. Their mission statements focus on connecting and empowering people, helping individuals accomplish their dreams, and creating a brighter future.

Today's five largest companies all touch the customer directly, which is a shift from the past. A century ago, the five largest companies were commodities and utilities (U.S. Steel, AT&T, Standard Oil, Bethlehem Steel, and Armour & Co.). Fifty years ago, manufacturers joined the ranks of the top five (IBM, AT&T, Eastman Kodak, General Motors, Standard Oil). Today's leaderboard—Apple, Alphabet, Microsoft, Amazon, and Facebook—are all service providers (accepting that some also produce hardware) and have direct relationships with their customers.

In this sense, Stephen's lessons apply to every industry. How will you make your guest feel welcome, relaxed, and wanting to spend more time with you? How will you ensure she or he returns and visits again? These questions apply as much to a social media company as they do to a timeshare. As Stephen observes, "We're all in hospitality now."

Even before most of these companies existed, Stephen was honing the rulebook they'd later need to follow. His mission was always much more grand than building a profitable timeshare business. He wanted to change the world by changing an entire industry and creating a new level of excellence to which all subsequent companies would aspire. As he relates in *Checking In*, a few bad actors have damaged the industry with their short-term thinking. After all, high-pressure sales tactics can lead a customer into a transaction that makes no sense. And when that deal blows up, which it almost inevitably will, it's not only the customer who suffers but also the company and, ultimately, the industry.

In the timeshare business, relationships with owners are measured in years and decades. Constant effort is required to maintain trust and a consistent level of quality and service. Doing so at one property is challenging—doing it across more than four hundred destinations in thirty-five countries on six continents is so difficult that it's effectively impossible.

It's no surprise, then, to read about Stephen's demanding schedule and constant travel to instill his values in the teams who operate Diamond Resorts' global properties. It only works if those teams feel a sense of ownership for their resorts, if they view their work as part of a bigger mission.

Which brings me to my closing point. For the past decade, the Milken Institute has focused on what will happen as the world enters a new age of employment in which increasing numbers of jobs are automated or augmented by robotics, artificial intelligence, and mechanical learning. Why does this matter? Because most of us derive great meaning and purpose from the work we do. Our most recent events have sought to address these challenges under the broader theme of "Building Meaningful Lives."

As the great Russian novelist Fyodor Dostoevsky explained: "Deprived of meaningful work, men and women lose their reason for existence; they go stark, raving mad." Such talk probably didn't make Fyodor a great dinner companion, but his point is well taken. We won't solve the "future of work" challenge in the remaining paragraphs of this foreword, but I will tie it back to Stephen.

Ask a happy employee what he or she does for a living, and you'll get a response filled with purpose. Even if they occupy what seems to be a mundane role, they're aware that they're part of something larger and are making the world better. Ask an unhappy worker the same question, and the answer will likely be along the lines of "gotta pay the bills" or "it's a living."

The difference again comes back to leadership, and in Stephen's case, I would argue the degree of difficulty is tremendous, in terms of the number of employees across different cultures and the range of jobs that all need to be operating in harmony to make a timeshare resort function well. How do you get all of those workers to feel that they should go above and beyond for the company?

Stephen is a master communicator with a rare knack for understanding and working with individuals across a wide range of functions—from the landscape, maintenance, and kitchen staff who mostly work behind the scenes to the front desk, wait staff, and valets who interact with customers. (To get a sense of this, go watch him on *Undercover Boss*.) This is the secret sauce of Stephen's success—and thereby the source of Diamond Resorts' success. Stephen cares about his workers and empowers them to take ownership and pride in their efforts. He makes sure they find meaning in their work. He earns their respect by placing his confidence in them, and they repay him by delivering world-class service.

And so it goes that when Stephen and I were chatting a year ago, he mentioned working on the book you're about to read. He asked if I would write a few words at the beginning to help set the tone, and only one word came to mind.

*Yes!*

**Michael Milken**
*Santa Monica, California*
*March 2018*

W hen I set out into this uncharted territory of writing a book, I asked an acquaintance of mine, who happens to be a three-time published author, for much-needed help.

"I'm trying to write a book about the *one* piece of advice successful business leaders of tomorrow need to know. As a successful author, what's the *one* tip you would give me about writing a book?"

He didn't hesitate. He didn't waver.

"You'll never go wrong treating the reader as you, yourself, would like to be treated."

Well, future reader, if you're anything like me, patience has never been a virtue.

So let's skip the pleasantries.

Let's skip the prologue.

Let's get right to brass tacks.

I've spent my entire career, my entire life, in hospitality. You name it, I've done it. Back of house, front of house, running the whole house. At the risk of getting ahead of myself, the company I would ultimately found—Diamond Resorts International—today has a network of hundreds of vacation destinations on six continents: that's covering the United States, Canada, Mexico, the Caribbean, South America, Central America, Europe, Asia, Australia, and Africa. In 2015, Diamond Resorts, which rose from the ashes of a predecessor nearly twice bankrupt, reported a healthy $954 million in revenue with a profit of, give or take, $150 million.[1] As we go to print, Diamond Resorts International is among the largest timeshare resort companies in the world—competing with the likes of Marriott, RCI, and Hilton—and is poised to grow.[2]

Mine isn't a rags-to-riches drama, but it is a true, practical, and instructive story about what it takes to find business success on your terms—nobody else's. My story is about what it takes to get ahead when everyone else is trying just to keep up, what it's like to see your business and career dreams go from tangled confusion to clear vision to reality.

> True leadership is about taking a stand for the people, principles, and products you believe in. Leadership is hollow without ownership.

It's only right that I warn you now: I built my business by breaking all the traditional rules, and I plan to write my book the very same way. You'll never hear me apologize for my successes or, for that matter, my failures, of which there are plenty. That's because true leadership is about taking a stand for the people, principles, and, yes, products you believe in—not shirking from them. I've learned that leadership is hollow without ownership.

I never saw myself writing a book of any kind, let alone a business book—and most certainly not a memoir. But I believe that sometimes we need to check in with ourselves, to figure out again what we're about, where we want to go, and how best to get there. I believe when we take a good, hard look at who we are as people and what we have to offer, we can do something powerful that changes our personal and professional outcomes. So what follows in the ensuing pages aren't watered-down stories, PC commentary, or self-help incantations. You won't get that from me. What follows are the once-in-a-lifetime experiences, career-defining moments, and hard-earned lessons you get only by rolling up your sleeves, diving in, and never looking back. What follows are strategies and stories that will make you think and definitively change how you approach people, problems, and possibilities.

## An Unconventional Path

I've never been a conventional business leader. I tell you this with a mixture of pride and humility. I didn't go to an Ivy League university or get my MBA. I never felt comfortable confined to a corner office. Everything that screams "executive" in the public imagination, it just wasn't me. Never has been, never will be.

I never was a traditional business leader, in part because I never had a traditional business education. Rather than interning in financial houses or Fortune 500 offices, I did my training in research laboratories and hospital autopsy rooms. (More on this later.) But ultimately, I found my way to the hotel industry, where I didn't just learn about hospitality, I was asked to live it; I didn't just memorize hospitality principles, I mastered them. And as I continue to watch new businesses in all sectors, in all corners of the globe, take shape today, I've learned to predict with staggering accuracy which of them will eventually flop and which of them will eventually soar, based on how well each internalizes the principles of hospitality into its culture, its code of conduct, and its core offerings.

Consider this: As of May 2018, the five biggest American companies by market value would all be tech companies—Apple at approximately $935 billion, Alphabet (the parent company of Google) at approximately $719 billion, Microsoft at $724 billion, Amazon at $765 billion, and Facebook at $515 billion.[3] That's an unprecedented, historic, consequential first, unmatched even in the dotcom era. This straightforward market truth suggests that the most vital challenges in business today orbit around technological change; and the companies that excel at breeding it, incorporating it, or acclimatizing to it are the ones reaping the biggest marketplace rewards.

But that's only *part* of the story. When creation and erasure happen with single keystrokes, and razor-precise efficiency becomes table stake, not a differentiator, what separates the companies that succeed from those that don't *isn't* technological edge on its own but rather a deeper sense of purpose, a clearer vision of the future, and a more eternal value proposition for those who matter most. What separates these companies from the rest is their focus on end users. On human beings. On people like us.

Technology efficiency, at the existential level, really isn't the full equation. Look at these corporate mission statements:

- Apple: "To make a contribution to the world by making tools for the mind that advance humankind."[4] (Steve Jobs's original mission statement for Apple.)
- Google: "To organize the world's information and make it universally accessible and useful."[5]
- Microsoft: "To empower every person and every organization on the planet to achieve more."[6]
- Amazon: "To be earth's most customer-centric company."[7]
- Facebook: "To give people the power to build community and bring the world closer together."[8]

We have the five biggest companies on the face of the planet today, all of which rely on state-of-the-art technology to run their products, programs, and platforms to drive their profits . . . and yet, there's no mention of the *t* word anywhere. When today's technology titans self-define who they are and what sets them apart from the competition, the absence of any nod to technology processes speaks volumes. Their mission statements instead speak to a clear-eyed understanding of fundamental human needs: truth, community, agency, growth, care.

What can we learn from the mission statements of the world's leading companies, all of which were created in the past fifty years and three of which were founded in only the last twenty-five years? First, that the powers behind these atmospheric success stories all stand for results, not process. Their greatness isn't foremost about *how* they develop new tools and treatments, but *why*. There is purpose because these companies have identified intrinsic human needs—the hunger for information, the desire for creativity, the need for connection, the pull toward progress—that they've set out to fill in their own way, on their own terms.

At the core, that's not technology. That's *hospitality*.

If we can argue that Apple, Alphabet, Facebook, Microsoft, and Amazon are all in the hospitality business—the business of taking care of fundamental human needs—it's not a far leap to this book's central premise: that no matter what industry you're in, no matter what personal goals you have as business leaders, entrepreneurs, dreamers, and doers, we're *all* in hospitality now.

That's what the following pages will seek to unspool: how the most successful businesses and business leaders of tomorrow will be moved by hospitality-driven thinking, even—or rather, *especially*—if they're not in the hospitality sector.

> No matter what industry you're in, no matter what personal goals you have as business leaders, entrepreneurs, dreamers, and doers, we're *all* in hospitality.

In its narrowest interpretation, the US travel and tourism industry (a common umbrella label for hospitality services as they're traditionally understood) generated more than $1.5 trillion in economic output in 2016 and supported 7.6 million US jobs. Hospitality exports accounted for 11 percent of all US exports and 33 percent of all US services exports, making travel and tourism the nation's largest services export. And one out of every eighteen Americans is employed, either directly or indirectly, in a travel or tourism-related industry.[9]

The preceding figures are significant, no doubt. But these conventional understandings of hospitality pale in comparison to the broader explanation I'd like to offer.

Allow me to be clear: What I *don't* mean to suggest with this central theme is that the world is moving to a place where we all work in accommodations and lodging, travel and transport, and food service (although, to be fair, each of these three subsectors are booming in their own right). What I *do* aim to imply is that the values long associated with and prioritized by these hospitality industries and in these sorts of traditional hospitality occupations are steadily increasing in importance, esteem, and, frankly, worth in every line of business.

So, what are values of hospitality? How does taking care of others translate into the competitive gains, first-movers' advantages, and strategic insights? To do hospitality right—to be genuine in our motivations and approaches—I think we need to have a clear understanding of what it's actually about and how it affects work and life. Then we can see what it might look like in our personal contexts, how to apply it, and how it really can change everything.

## The Principles of Hospitality

I've found that the concept of hospitality hinges upon five key pillars. These pillars not only impact the way I view people but also inform my approach to business. When I act on these principles, allowing them to drive my decisions,

I believe I communicate to people that they matter, which is something that always positively affects the outcome. It's also the right thing to do.

## THE FIRST PRINCIPLE OF HOSPITALITY: FOCUS UNRELENTINGLY ON THE GUEST

In my industry—timeshare—the guest I'm talking about is literal. But what about in another industry, like technology? In this case, your guest is your website visitor, your software user—not the advertiser or marketer whose ads flank the pages. In finance? The guest is whomever is trusting the financial institution to safely guard their hard-earned resources. In education? Guests are not the lobbyists or the reformers, not the administrators or even the parents, but the students, the pupils who get one shot at the quality K–12 experience they deserve. In health care? Not the experts, not the doctors, not the pharmaceutical companies, but the patients.

When viewed through the lens of hospitality, every trade has a guest. In times of crisis and confusion, of opportunity and openings, success starts with correctly identifying and staying steadfastly loyal to your guest. And real hospitality—the kind that makes a lasting impact—calls for an unrelenting focus on the guest.

> When viewed through the lens of hospitality, every trade has a guest.

## THE SECOND PRINCIPLE OF HOSPITALITY: COMMIT TO CONTINUOUS IMPROVEMENT

An unrelenting emphasis on the guest means never being satisfied with current offerings. This second hospitality value pivots on the idea of always reaching for higher, reaching for more, reaching for better. It's the slow, steady rejection of complacency, not out of fear that competitors will out-pace you but out of the genuine, generous belief that there's still more you can do, still more you can offer.

An unrelenting emphasis on the guest means never being satisfied with current offerings.

## THE THIRD PRINCIPLE OF HOSPITALITY: PRIORITIZE REPUTATION OVER BRAND

As you look for better, smarter, more meaningful ways to bring the optimum to others around you, the third hospitality principle comes into play. You'll need to think about who you are, what you're about, what you're building, and who you're doing that with.

I've never understood why so many companies today are obsessed with "branding." Branding is what your hired spokespeople, your paid-for advertising, your preplanned marketing says about you. But a focus on reputation means you're listening to—and learning from—what your guests, your customers, your stakeholders, even your competitors and your critics have to say. Frankly, as a business owner, there's no one I'd rather hear from more. Prioritizing reputation over brand means you care more about what others think of you than what you have to say about yourself. It forces you to prioritize the health of your organization from the inside out.

Prioritizing reputation over brand means you care more about what others think of you than what you have to say about yourself.

## THE FOURTH PRINCIPLE OF HOSPITALITY: ENSURE TOTAL ALIGNMENT

The fourth value of hospitality, total alignment, is easy to suggest but much harder to achieve. When more companies are going not just international, but multinational (in terms of supply chain, service delivery, and customer base), how do you keep the experience of your product and service consistent while adapting to the unique needs of different people and places, inevitable setbacks, and unforeseen events? How do you ensure that leadership from the top is complemented and matched by grassroots leadership throughout the organization? How do you keep a team of two or a team of two hundred thousand focused on the same goals, delivering the same quality results, in the same signature style?

I've found that one way to achieve this is to stay focused on doing what it takes to do right by the customer and allowing this to set your path. This part of the book shows you how I tackled the issue of total alignment in my organization and what I learned from it. While you may not approach things exactly as I did, these underlying concepts can and should inform your day-to-day decisions.

> Do what it takes to do right by the customer.

## THE FIFTH PRINCIPLE OF HOSPITALITY: DO WELL BY DOING GOOD

Finally, the fifth and last hospitality value is as much a signature trademark as it is a defining principle: doing good for others as you do well for yourself. The most successful among us in hospitality never see our work as a "job." Rather, we see it as a calling. To take care of one another in a way that's uniquely suited to our needs isn't transactional but innately and intimately personal. There's no escaping it—and that's a good thing.

A teacher with a passion for educating in motion at the blackboard—that's a full expression of hospitality.

A doctor who's not just treating a child's illness but seeing and healing the whole individual—that's a full expression of hospitality.

A chef caring about the selection of each ingredient on a plate to bring a meal to its highest form for a diner he may never meet—that's a full expression of hospitality.

A certain first-time writer doing his utmost to treat future readers with the same respect, care, and generosity he'd like to be treated with himself—that's a full expression of hospitality.

> To take care of one another in a way that's uniquely suited to our needs isn't transactional but innately and intimately personal.

When you're able to connect the effort, labor, and intensity of your hard work to another person's benefit—however many steps removed, however far the impact extends—that's doing good for others as you do well for yourself. The rewards of finding your way to "work in hospitality" have a multiplier effect that ricochets among business, customer, and community.

## The Meaning of Yes

Once you're focused on your guests, committed to continuously offering them improved experiences, prioritizing your reputation over your branding, practicing total alignment across your spheres of influence, and doing good for others while doing well for yourself, you'll begin to see not only how the pillars buttress one another but also how the power of hospitality can be a boon in any business. As business leaders, entrepreneurs, and change agents, the question for us then becomes: How do we bring these ideals, principles, and values to life in our own way?

I suggest starting with a single word: *Yes.*

*Yes* to challenges, *yes* to (smart) risk, *yes* to making a difference. *Yes* to taking on more responsibility (not just because you can but because you should). *Yes* to partaking in something bigger than yourself. *Yes* to setting the example you hope others will emulate. *Yes* to not just teaching but also to learning from those who work for you and with you. *Yes* to putting principles and people over profit as you discover, all the while, how prioritizing *values* is the cornerstone of your business's bottom-line value.

The Meaning of Yes is a philosophy I came up with that's based on a radical customer service mind-set. It became the mantra and mantle of Diamond Resorts International. It became our way of distilling the full meaning of hospitality across continents, time zones, and language divides into a single word—*yes*—that everyone everywhere immediately recognized, fully comprehended, and inherently appreciated.

Today, everyone who works for Diamond Resorts International—from front desk staff to valet to CEO—intuitively understands what the Meaning of Yes is all about and what it calls on each and every one of us to do: go above and beyond for our guests without hesitation, reserve, or calculation.

The business graveyard is littered with too many unfortunate examples of penny-wise, pound-foolish models that prioritize short-term concerns—saying no to long-term value. In fact, if you pick up your newspaper right now, I have no doubt that the front page of the business section won't be celebrating a CEO's success but rather needling his or her unforced errors. I guarantee you the foul was made because the individual decided sales and financial projections were more important than what their core constituents deserve here and now, that some other objective was more important than living up to the demands of hospitality. The names change, the details vary, but the root cause is always the same.

CEOs, brands, and businesses become notorious when they flunk this simple test: Do you believe in your products, your goods, your services so much that you can say yes to what your customers and your team members are asking for? All too often in business—and in life—the wrong decisions come from nothing but insecurity: a lack of confidence to say what you mean, mean what you say, and (the most critical part) follow through not just in words but in action.

This book is committed to explaining the core pillars of hospitality that make up the Meaning of Yes, a deceptively simple idea with huge implications for our work, our businesses, and our futures. I don't claim to have reached the conclusions presented in the following pages on my own. Far from it. My opinions about business, relationships, and strategic financial risks haven't been formed in isolation. I've had the privilege to learn from—and test these lessons with—the very best. Among them are American financier and global philanthropist Mike Milken; the steadfast Senator Harry Reid; GOP consultant and master wordsmith Frank Luntz; the all-too-humble CEO and chairman of MGM Resorts International Jim Murren; sage and patient Linda Nordstrom; the inimitable Roger Dow; and many others for whom the dictionary lacks sufficient superlatives. They will make appearances throughout this book in anecdotes and in sharing peerless advice no MBA program or textbook can give.

For my part, I forged my path in the vacation-ownership industry; but the Meaning of Yes and the pillars of hospitality it represents are relevant to anyone, in any field, with dreams of shaking up the status quo to succeed on their own terms.

> This book is committed to explaining the core pillars of hospitality that make up the Meaning of Yes, a deceptively simple idea with huge implications for our work, our businesses, and our futures.

So, in an effort to treat you as I'd like to be treated, reader, here is what I can promise you about what comes next: Every story contained in these pages is 100 percent true; every business observation shared is designed to be both impactful and immediately actionable in your own life; and every bit of it is totally unexpected.

've built this book around pivotal life lessons, key experiences, and business perspectives that have meaningfully impacted and defined my success, all of it intended to provide you with the practical business and motivational insights you need to define your own success. When it comes down to it, whatever path you're currently on, whatever industry you're in, whatever role you have, you'll see that we're all on this journey together and that as you consider living the principles of hospitality presented in this book, we have the opportunity to collaborate and achieve something truly great.

## Part One

The first portion of *Checking In* details the path I walked, setting out on my journey to becoming CEO and founder of Diamond Resorts International.

How did someone who declared premed in college and ambled through internships in the unlikeliest of places—including the hospital autopsy room (I kid you not)—end up building the first permanent timeshare property in Las Vegas? How did someone with no formal business training wind up starting a company at the age of twenty-five and then go on to sell *another* business to lodging-industry giant Marriott? How did an average boy from an average family with an average upbringing grow up to not only found thriving businesses but also change the course of an entire industry along the way?

In this portion of the book, you'll find a frank series of portraits of some of the biggest role models in my life. I do this to probe the advice they shared that took my life in new directions, offer a meditation on the missteps I made along the way, and show you how these insights and experiences might inform you on your own journey.

If there's anything I learned while reflecting on the life and decisions that led me to Diamond Resorts, it's that the course to success never follows a straight line. There are misdirections and stopgaps, periods of procrastination, and outright blunders. But those trials make us stronger and wiser. Those trials highlight our humanity and develop our compassion. And those trials make it all worthwhile. (As they say, you only fail if you give up.)

> **If there's anything I learned while reflecting on the life and decisions that led me to Diamond Resorts, it's that the course to success never follows a straight line.**

There's a professor by the name of Adam Grant at the Wharton School of the University of Pennsylvania whose work I strongly admire. Even if you don't know him by name, you've likely been affected by his ideas and body of work. He's one of Malcolm Gladwell's self-professed favorite thinkers. He's received praise from Sir Richard Branson of the Virgin Group. He's collaborated with Sheryl Sandberg. Point being, Grant is a tried-and-true thought leader. Some of his latest studies delve into the world of what he calls *originals*—what the rest of us would call *entrepreneurs who've made it.*

In short, Grant examines the traits of people who've changed the world through their ingenuity and willingness to do things differently. And what did he find? That these "originals" have doubt, fear, and failures, just like you and me. They procrastinate and take wrong turns. They have *bad* ideas (and plenty of them). But what sets these originals, these entrepreneurs—or whatever you want to call them—apart is a gritty, crazy, inexplicable willingness to stomach risk, take chances, and chase after the unconventional ideas that other people are too sensible to bet on.

> ## We're all capable of big things, if we just have the tenacity to pursue them.

My purpose in telling you all this? What's special about my upbringing is, well, nothing at all. You'll see that I had a handful of decent ideas—and far more terrible ones. I dealt with typical anxiety and doubt. I fell on my face. I walked down several wildly different paths before finding the right one for me. But I believe we're all capable of big things, if we just have the tenacity to pursue them.

But what I hope you discern most of all in my story is a reflection of yourself. Where are you in life as you read this? I want my story to push you to take stock of who *you* are today and think about where you want to go.

## Part Two

The second section of the book details my time at the helm of Diamond Resorts International, from its darkest days in the wake of the 2008 financial crisis to the time I helped redefine an industry, all contrasted against the backdrop of five key pillars of hospitality. My aim in these chapters is to bring to life the strategic decision making that built Diamond Resorts, along with the resulting outcomes. In these chapters, you'll find clear takeaways and parallels from me and others that you can apply to not only thorny and tricky business situations but also to regular daily life.

## Part Three

Part three details how transformative principles of hospitality—and the corresponding Meaning of Yes—are instrumental beyond building a business; they're instrumental in changing careers, exceeding expectations in personal and professional life, and positively shaking up the political status quo. From the transformation of Las Vegas from trading post to international destination to the chartering of an experimental government initiative designed to bolster tourism and the US economy as a whole, part three is about viewing leadership through the lens of hospitality.

## Part Four

And in part four, I do my best to impart the encouragement, guidance, and proposals that I wholly believe will differentiate and define the business opportunities of the future.

• • •

I've been blessed to lead an interesting life, but I'll count my blessings double if I can pass along some of the lessons I've learned. Some I figured out the hard way; others I've fought hard *for*. I hope you'll take the sum of all this and go on to realize your goals.

What are you waiting for? It's time to check in.

# PART ONE

# Beginnings

Like many American families, mine came from humble roots. My grandfather, Jacob "Itchkie" Cloobeck, came from Belarus to settle in Chicago in the early 1900s with nothing in his pockets, no money to his name, no acquaintances or relatives to call on. He did carry with him the American dream: an aspiration to fashion a better life for himself, his family, and his posterity by going as far as his talents would take him.

It's a common story, but I wonder today if it's one we still believe as a country. We should. Our shared faith in the idea of the American dream is what makes it possible in the first place.

Itchkie's Chicago was the stuff of legend: Factories mixed with crowded tenant housing, squalor alongside resplendent wealth, seas of people from every corner of the world going in every direction. He made ends meet by selling vegetables and fruit from a cart to local households and workers. Personable, persevering, and known for his sonorant voice that called housewives from their kitchens, the neighborhood dubbed him "the watermelon king of Chicago." Soon his hand-pushed cart flourished into a full-fledged produce business.

I start my story with Itchkie's because hearing his was my first exposure to the idea that life is what you make it. He came with nothing, and against the backdrop of 1920s Chicago—which itself was rapidly transforming from a regional trading outpost in the heartland of the United States into one of the country's largest cities[1]—built a business his family would be proud of. I know I certainly am.

When I was six, my father clipped our family from its Chicago beginnings and moved us to a neighborhood located in the San Fernando Valley's outer suburbs of Los Angeles, California. (I blame the move for my everlasting aversion to temperatures that dip below fifty degrees.) My father had made a career for himself in real estate with a company by the name of World Leisure Time. He may have been in a different industry, but he still carried Itchkie's entrepreneurial streak. As a partner with the firm, he helped the company develop a revolutionary product for the time: land lots for sale.

In our family, listening to the ads that blasted the radio and television airwaves about these dream lots was a daily ritual at the time. This was always accompanied by a smile of pride from my father, no matter how hard he tried to keep a straight face. From hearing about Itchkie to watching my father, I came to equate work with pride, and pride with work. Yes, it was clearly a means of providing, but it was also a source of internal dignity and happiness for them both.

And so, ignoring child labor laws, I started my first job at the age of eight. I became a busboy at Brooktrails Lodge, one of my father's properties.

## My First Job

These summers were some of the fondest of my childhood. I always went to the kitchen early to hear the older waiters and cooks talk among themselves—about yesterday's work, about their personal lives, about anything at all. Maybe it was because I was the boss's son, but they never chided me. Instead, they included me. In listening to their chatter, I felt part of a team, part of a purpose, and part of something bigger than myself.

Anyone who's ever worked in a kitchen knows just how chaotic back-of-the-house operations can be: the roaring stovetops, the billowing smoke, the rapid chopping of knives, the swarming of impatient staff trying to satiate the even more impatient customers. That I was not only holding my own but also contributing to this nonstop operation made me feel like I had figured out the world of adults. When I was clearing plates and washing dishes, I wasn't a kid; I was an important part of the crew.

Maybe it was the sense of involvement, maybe it was the treats the cooks would sneak me every so often, or maybe it was the paycheck that made me swell with self-esteem every two weeks. Regardless, I realized I loved working and earning my own way.

I can't reminisce over Brooktrails and not mention Lucille. Lucille was a powerhouse of a woman who commanded the restaurant's kitchen with unquestionable authority and unmatched know-how. Somehow, even as she was already overworked, dishing out instructions to her staff, supervising the quality of the cooking, and managing inventory, she found time to take me under her wing. With her diligent, patient help, I mastered the art—and it truly is an art—of perfectly fried bacon and lighter-than-air pancakes.

But Lucille taught me more than cooking. Through her example, she taught me that a true leader makes others feel welcome, not wary. She built people up and in so doing made her team better than just the sum of its parts. It's a lesson that has stuck with me for decades and has become a central component of the Meaning of Yes.

A true leader makes others feel welcome, builds people up, and in so doing, makes a team better than just the sum of its parts.

Summer after summer, through middle school and high school, I returned to Brooktrails Lodge—as a dishwasher, as an assistant cook, as a maintenance worker, as housekeeping staff. There was nothing I wouldn't do. And this, in retrospect, was the most valuable education I ever received.

## What School Taught Me

By the fall of 1979, I was off to college. After a year at USC, I transferred to Brandeis University in Boston, which only confirmed my suspicions that I have no appreciation for the cold. A good Jewish boy from a good Jewish middle-class family, I knew that now it was time to choose a life for myself. I had all of three options: (1) become a rabbi, (2) become a lawyer, or (3) become a doctor.

I declared premed.

Brandeis was, and continues to be, a fine liberal arts institution with a theological bent. Approximately 80 percent of my peers were Jewish social science majors: history, the humanities, literature, language, political science. As I recall, there were little to no business offerings, but its budding science program held promise. At the time, Brandeis boasted an 83 percent admittance rate to medical schools—not a detail to be overlooked.

My head was down and my nose buried deep in biology and chemistry textbooks. But no matter how hard I studied or how much I read, my grades hit a hard ceiling I could not break through: At my very best, my academic performance was mediocre.

Here's my senior year transcript to prove it.

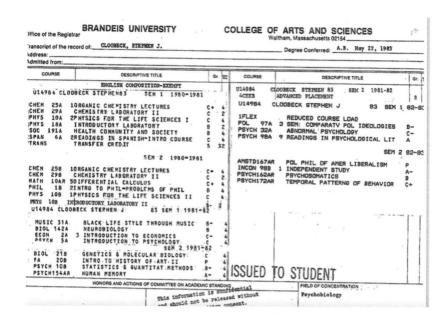

Stephen Cloobeck's college transcript.

In fact, the marks shown here are admittedly inflated. I remember honing my negotiation skills by visiting professors after hours, persuading them to alter my Ds to C minuses, my C minuses to Cs, and so on. This is not a system I would recommend to any students perusing these pages today; but for me, it was enough to scrape by.

I graduated in 1983, never truly content with the idea that my potential was captured by my academic performance. Years later, I would receive a clarifying diagnosis. Despite completing a full K–12 education and four years of college training, it turns out I had been dyslexic the entire time.

I never once suspected.

## Dyslexia

Dyslexia is a loosely applied umbrella term for disorders that involve difficulty in learning to read or interpret words, letters, and symbols. Emerging studies show that dyslexics rely on complicated decision-making pathways in the brain, which are often revealed in more creative problem solving and strategic thinking. This makes sense to me intuitively; I know for certain the struggles I faced in my youth contributed to the successes I found in my adulthood.

Some might call dyslexia a disability, but in my life and my business it's proven to be an asset. I see things that others don't. I make connections that others can't. I imagine possibilities that others wouldn't dream of.

In high school, for example, I remember growing increasingly disappointed—if not downright discouraged—that all those hours I spent studying for quizzes and tests, sweating over homework assignments, and attending after-school study groups had only resulted in lackluster grades. I knew how hard I was working. I knew that I grasped the concepts and lessons. But I didn't know why I wasn't seeing scores that reflected the effort I was putting into learning.

To me, there *had* to be a better way. I reasoned that if I couldn't work harder, maybe I could work smarter. At one point, I set out on a solo visit to the town's bookstore. Instead of going to the student or self-help section, I marched directly to the teacher manuals and guides. If I couldn't learn from the student study guides, I figured there must be something in the way teachers prepared themselves that could help me.

Jackpot.

Opening a manual to chemistry, I noticed that the "template tests" in the back of the book matched every exam a certain tenured teacher of mine had given that year. Not only that, there were template tests for upcoming lessons. Suddenly, the answers were right there, staring me in the face—they were *actually* staring me in the face. Immediately, I snapped the book closed and proceeded to the cashier. I ordered a book for myself and kept the receipt, which wound up being a good thing.

Almost overnight, my Ds and Cs went to straight As—nearly perfect marks. My school was naturally interested in this about-face in performance. Had it been the afternoon help? The extra homework they'd given me? Some kind of change at home? I shook my head no and proudly produced the teacher's manual from my book bag.

It didn't go over quite as well as I imagined.

The praise I'd expected for seeking out more "effective" study habits and resources was swiftly replaced with a scolding, suspension, and near expulsion. Luckily, by producing the receipt I had saved when I purchased the book, I could prove that I didn't "cheat"; I had just used all the resources at my disposal. (Actually, the teacher was reprimanded more than I was. It turns out you're only supposed to use teaching manuals as a guide and not a color-by-numbers replacement.)

When I look back on all this, I realize that what teachers would have labeled as a handicap in school became a strategic advantage in my life. And so I pass on some of my learning to you: If one path doesn't work, find another. I didn't go the traditional route; I went my own way.

## ADDRESS. ASSESS. ACT.

I had one professor in college who did me a great favor: She never mistook test scores for capability. She was none other than Margret Rey, coauthor of the *Curious George* children's books. True to her main character's moniker, Professor Rey applauded curiosity, not rote learning; problem solving, not prerequisites. She had a supremely uncanny knack for fascinating students with her lectures, which always felt more like stories you wanted to listen to and be enraptured by than lesson periods you *had* to attend. She was an author, after all, and made her points by illustration, not declaration.

If there was one moral to Margret Rey's work, it was this: When you encounter a problem, which we all do from time to time, you address it, you assess it, and then you act on it.

To this day, I credit Professor Rey for teaching me how to think about problems, choices, and life. She impacted the way I would later go on to approach situations and engage with others. I wonder how differently my career would have gone had I not learned this lesson early on. And so I pass this on to you.

> Address. Assess. Act.
>    Not making any decision often leaves you worse off than making the wrong choice in the first place.

## YES TO ANY ASSIGNMENT

My premed direction meant finding appropriate apprenticeships to complement my coursework. To be close to family, I spent summers in California, interning at a Cedars-Sinai research facility, assisting with endocrinological programs and tests. Again, I was part of a team, doing significant work that held the promise of real-world importance and impact. The equipment may have been a bit pricier and the food hall less appetizing, but, in a way, I felt like I was back in the kitchen.

Like any good doctor-in-training, I spent time in one research lab, practiced in a new clinical environment, and then moved on to the next. I remember being ecstatic to begin an internship at Cedars-Sinai Medical Center in Los Angeles. In my mind, I was well on the road to becoming a world-class surgeon, and that's when I recalled what I had learned at Brooktrails Lodge: Good things come to those willing to work longer and harder than anyone else at the jobs no one wants to take. I resolved to say yes to any assignment.

Frankly, I never once imagined that they'd stick me in a *hospital autopsy room,* though. Those nights I spent in the mortuary played no small role in the premature end of my medical career. Suffice it to say, I discovered I was more of a people person—an *alive*-people person. But the lesson remains the same:

> Good things come to those willing to work longer and harder than anyone else at the jobs no one wants to take.

I knew I had a good work ethic. And I knew I would go on to do something more.

## GETTING SCHOOLED

My time in the autopsy room aside, I could see at some point that there were some emerging signs that a fissure was growing between what I thought I *should* do and what I *wanted* to do. I was no longer sure I wanted to pursue my original career path. If not medicine, then naturally, I thought my calling should be law. (Let's just say that even then, I knew I didn't have the disposition to be a rabbi.) So, my senior year at Brandeis, I made a 180-degree turn, registered for the LSAT, and applied to law school.

But when acceptance letters arrived, I felt none of the excitement, none of the purpose that I remembered so fondly from my early days at Brooktrails Lodge. How could it be that this wasn't right, either?

I didn't know what I wanted to do; I just knew I didn't want to spend my days in an office, kept company by briefs, legal texts, and impenetrable judicial decisions and corporate contracts. It all just seemed so . . . *regimented.* I envisioned where I'd be in three years after taking the bar: in a clerkship at a firm whose letterhead was the compiled list of founding partners' surnames.

But where was the adventure?

Where was the excitement?

Where was the opportunity to do something no one had ever accomplished before?

Like many young graduates I talk to today, I had a diploma but not a clue. I didn't know *what* I wanted to do with my life.

And having just finished financing four years of my college tuition at the time, my dad was none too pleased about this. Since I didn't have a sense of direction, he made sure to provide one for me. He called me home, to Las Vegas in those days, to learn his newest revolutionary innovation in real estate: timeshare.

## The Final Word

- Good things come to those willing to work longer and harder than anyone else.

- There's something about being part of a team and contributing to a purpose that's bigger than yourself.

- By building up others, you make any team you're on better than the sum of its parts.

- Address. Assess. Act. Not making a decision often leaves you worse off than making the *wrong* decision.

- When there's a divide between what you think you *should* do and what you *want* to do, reflect. Think about what you're passionate about. Think about your experiences so far. Think about what success means to you—no one else. And when you've thought through your options, my advice to you: Bet on yourself. If you don't, who will?

# Striking Out on My Own

I built my success on the timeshare industry. It wasn't easy, it involved great personal risk and sacrifice, and I stumbled plenty along the way. Still, core lessons I'd learned from my family, my early jobs, and my academic career stayed with me, and I often counted on that early wisdom to keep me grounded. Today, I'm probably most known in the business world for the way I helped reinvent and redefine the timeshare industry, but I hope, however, that you'll see me as someone who's worked hard to make something bigger than that, as someone who advocates for authentic hospitality in every sphere of influence. This is the story of my journey, as it begins in real estate.

## A Truncated History of Timeshare

Timeshare may be a taken-for-granted part of vacationers' lexicon today, like it's always been an option, but it certainly wasn't awhile ago. So that you understand how I got to where I am in business today, let me offer you a short history of the concept before I get into the nitty-gritty of my career path. As I share the details—both good and bad—I hope you'll see just how far time-share has come and how this set the scene for the Meaning of Yes.

## MAKING VACATIONS ACCESSIBLE

Depending on who you believe, the timeshare first got its start in Switzerland or France sometime in the late 1950s or early 1960s. But everyone agrees that the invention was designed by families, for families who wanted a better way to get away.

In Switzerland, an ordinary man by the name of Alexander Nette decided there *had* to be a way to incorporate regular holidays on his annual calendar. The barriers? Rent. Upkeep. Time. Even in the midcentury boom, holidays were expensive, a luxury that many regular families couldn't afford on their own, at least not annually.

I like to believe that the mantra "Necessity is the mother of all invention" holds true in Nette's case. Determined to find a way to make regular vacations more accessible to everyone, he teamed up with a business partner by the name of Dr. Guido M. Renggli and together, in the fall of 1963, they founded a company by the name of **H**otel- und **A**partmenthaus **I**mmobilien **A**nlage **AG** (Hapimag).[1] Immediately, the duo began to acquire resort properties. But here's the kicker: As opposed to traditional deeded real estate, Nette and Renggli marketed Hapimag as a new "right to use" share program. Not only was Hapimag the first timeshare operation to use a points program and offer its members different timeshare destinations, it's still a successful company to this day.

Nearly simultaneously, a French company by the name of Le Société des Grands Travaux de Marseille—quite a mouthful, even for the French—began selling at a ski resort in the French Alps. Their advertising mantra? "No need to rent the room; buy the hotel, it's cheaper!" Pretty catchy—it's no surprise it caught on.

## MAKING THE PRODUCT UNDERSTANDABLE

Timeshare was a bit slower to take off stateside, but once it did, it spread like wildfire. First there was a hotel-condominium project on the island of Maui, which broke ground in October 1965. Hawaii proved a wellspring for the timeshare industry, and shortly thereafter, another project arrived on the scene, the first non-hotel condo timeshare sold in the United States, on the island of Kauai. Founded by Bob Burns and Bob Ringenburg (dubbed the "two Bobs"), this small operation selling leasehold condos in weekly intervals became timeshare giant Vacation Internationale.

And that brings us to another great name of this generation, Brockway Springs, the first deeded timeshare program in the United States. Originally a single property opened in 1973 in Lake Tahoe, California, developer Innisfree Corporations grew its business, joining forces with Hyatt Corporation in a fifty-fifty joint venture led by industry legends Carl Berry, Paul Gray, Greg Bright, Doug Murdock, and Dave Irmer.

This group of men made *timeshare* a household term. Interestingly enough, their choice in words wasn't a stroke of marketing genius or the product of incessant message testing but rather a plain and direct attempt to make the product intuitive and understandable. Bankers, a major target audience, were already familiar with the term in their own business, as *timeshare* referred to the sharing of mainframe computers.[2]

## MAKING CUSTOMERS' DREAMS COME TRUE

By the 1970s, timeshare familiarity, construction, and purchasing had skyrocketed. The phenomenon was a confluence of push-pull factors: real estate developers having difficulty selling full-ownership condominiums in a down economy and the booming consumer popularity of the interval model.

I can't underscore this point enough: The introduction of the "mainstream vacation" appealed to people everywhere, with every level of economic means. The promise of a timeshare became synonymous with the dream of luxury getaways, reasonable prices, and mobility for all Americans.

## How a Reputation Is Ruined

Let's take a hypothetical example: Real estate developers realize they can't off-load their inventory. Perhaps it's a hotel, perhaps it's a condominium building, perhaps it's a string of homes in a gated area. Rather than admitting to a bust and losing everything, these developers would sometimes attempt to sell their properties piecemeal, in blocks of time, to keep creditors at bay and avoid defaulting on loans.

Let's say a condo developer built units that he was trying to sell for $200,000, but he couldn't find buyers willing to pay that price at that time. Alternatively, the developer could sell the condo for $20,000 per week, for each of the fifty weeks out of the year, and make $1,000,000. It was profitable, to say the least, if one doesn't factor in carrying costs, management fees, property maintenance, sales and marketing costs, cancellations, defaults, and the host of other expenses that many inexperienced timeshare developers often neglect to consider.

Given that deceptively wide margin, you can see how some might be tempted to hyperfocus on sales over genuine value. The faster these developers could sell weeks, the more quickly they could pay their lenders and make a handsome return. But this brings about poor practices, bad customer experiences, negative associations with timeshare sales, and the degradation of the industry as a whole. As you may guess, this is also the type of nearsightedness that leads to short-lived companies and industries.

Most of my readers can probably intuit the rest. By the 1990s, major hotel companies (including Marriott, Sheraton, Hyatt, Hilton, and others) began offering vacation-ownership properties. Today, add Starwood, Disney, and scores more to that list.

## MAKING IT ABOUT MORE THAN SALES

But as everyone knows—and this goes for any industry—all it takes is a few bad actors to spoil a reputation for everyone. A detail overlooked here, a consumer request denied there, cutting corners when no one's looking. It all adds up. And it didn't take long for the word *timeshare* to be tainted by preconceived notions of poor customer service, lackluster experiences, and a mass, generic feel overall.

Just thinking about it makes me mad, because I know how hard people like my father worked to deliver the original timeshare promise: special time out of the year designed just for you and your family to relax, explore, and live the good life, however you defined it, for a fair and affordable cost. Rather than delivering the Meaning of Yes, a few bad actors across the timeshare property landscape caused the term to become largely synonymous with no.

There's one unique factor about timeshare that made it particularly vulnerable to exploitation: its ceaseless focus on sales. The incessant urge of those in the industry to sell and compete with one another—accompanied by the zeal of new vacation possibilities without due oversight—brought about the unfortunate growth of sales tactics that were questionable at best and perhaps even illegal at worst.

Most states thankfully now have regulations that guard against high-pressure sales tactics. No one wants to be stuck with a property in perpetuity they hadn't fully thought out in one critical moment—it's not good for the consumer, not good for the company, and not good for the industry. Hilton, Starwood, Wyndham, and Diamond have persevered in the timeshare space because we all understand the inherent risk in it. This business is not for the faint of heart.

Again, I share this unfortunate history of timeshare with you to highlight how far the industry has come since. The oft-mocked bait-and-switch vacations of old are long gone. Although today, timeshare is a multibillion-dollar industry, I began my journey against the backdrop of all this.

## My Early Career

In real estate, I learned quickly that there were no guarantees, just gambles. In addition to the actual construction of a building, there was negotiation and relationship building, there was risk, and at the end of a successful project, there was reward.

Back then, anxious to prove myself on my own terms, I decided not to enlist in my father's budding business but rather to join a firm by the name of Independent Development Corporation. Here, as in every position I'd held before, I was the youngest person in the office but willing to do any job and work harder and longer than anyone else. I learned how to navigate leases, manage shopping centers, design a structure, and most important of all, supervise a project's construction. I was on-site on weekends, in hard hats on holidays, and working long hours in between. I knew this was necessary so

I could learn from my employees and tenants. It was a whole new education, and I was determined to follow the accelerated track.

> If only we'd be a little bit bolder, a little more aggressive, we could build more, do more, achieve more.

By the age of twenty-five, I'd had enough of working for someone else. I looked for other jobs, but even at different firms, I would still be playing by someone else's rules. If only we'd be a little bit bolder, a little more aggressive, we could build more, do more, achieve more. I knew there was opportunity, I just didn't know where to find it.

Then one day, a friend of the family, a man by the name of Ken Ruby, gave me a single piece of advice that set the rest of my life in motion: "Stephen. You're young. You're ambitious. And frankly, a little hotheaded. But you have nothing to lose. If you want to run a company your way, go start your own business."

That counsel was a revelation. Why *not* start an entirely new company? Why *not* take a risk? Why *not* bet on myself?

There was one problem. My father *recoiled* at the notion. His concerns were only natural. He worried about me taking on too much, too soon. He worried that I was too young, too inexperienced. He worried about what would happen if I failed. And why put myself through the anxiety and apprehension when I could simply work with him? Wasn't that the security he had worked so hard to provide?

> There will always be reasons *not* to start a company. The telltale sign of emerging entrepreneurs is not a once-in-a-generation idea or a perfected business plan, but the confidence to bet on themselves.

This was the first time I'd truly disappoint my dad. I went forward with my own business plan, against his wishes. I knew his worries were about my welfare; but I couldn't help but think: "If not now, when?" There will always be reasons *not* to start a company. The telltale sign of emerging entrepreneurs is not a once-in-a-generation idea or a perfected business plan, but the confidence to bet on themselves.

## MY FIRST COMPANY, A NEAR DISASTER

My first company was Commercial Center Development. A yawn-inducing name, I know. And the model was just as glamorous: We specialized in building and leasing shopping centers in and around California.

Most deals were good. A few were mediocre. And one, Lake Forest, was a calamity. It happened shortly after I set out on my own. I started what seemed to be a run-of-the-mill project in Southern California that turned out to be anything but. Midway through construction, my general contractor went bust. It was happening to a lot of businesses; the late 1980s saw a deep real estate recession. And one by one, I received phone calls from signed tenants saying they, too, were broke and would be reneging on their commitments.

I was up the proverbial creek without a builder and without the anticipated cash flow to make the mortgage payments when (and if) the center finished. To take this debacle from dismal to downright disastrous, my lender at the time went belly-up too. Savings and loans, both gone at the same time.

It began to look like my father's predictions of failure were materializing.

But there's no giving up before giving in. I realized that there was only one way out: step in and do the work myself. I rolled up my sleeves, took a deep breath, and picked up the tool belt. I built retaining walls. I installed flooring. I interpreted architectural blueprints. And through sweat, elbow grease, and sheer persistence, I took what was on paper and made it reality.

But even as I made the physical space work, I knew there was still the financial component to address. The project wouldn't be viable until, somehow, the numbers added up—and that meant re-leasing the space. Long days became long nights as I learned to advertise and market to potential tenants, courting them to see the possibilities that few others could.

Finally, the government stepped in. The Resolution Trust Corporation (RTC) was a government-owned asset management company run by Lewis William Seidman. Seidman was charged with liquidating assets, primarily real estate–related assets such as mortgage loans that had been assets of savings and loan associations declared insolvent by the Office of Thrift Supervision as a consequence of the savings and loan crisis of the 1980s. The RTC also took over the insurance functions of the former Federal Home Loan Bank Board.

Between 1989 and the middle of 1995, the RTC closed or otherwise resolved 747 thrifts with total assets of $394 billion. But luckily for me, the company was so disorganized at the outset that every time I prepared to work with them, a new case agent called. That bought time, and time bought clarity. In the end, the solution presented itself to me: I'd work out the debt in the form of transferring assets to the RTC—without penalty.

I had scraped by with bruises to my ego, finances, and reputation. But I never went bankrupt. I never let a single one of my contractors or subs down. I never reneged on my end of the bargain. Surviving that adversity was as formative an experience as I've ever had.

> **As hard as it was, this experience taught me about risk, the difference between what you *can* leverage and what you *should* leverage.**

In the coming years, I would allow the memories and lessons from the Lake Forest project to shape my outlook as both a builder and operator. I never would have understood architecture, structural engineering, mechanical systems, civil engineering, and day-to-day construction techniques had I not experienced my brush with disaster.

As hard as it was, this experience taught me about risk, the difference between what you *can* leverage and what you *should* leverage. It also confirmed *this* for me: If you're going to bet on something, you better bet on yourself.


## POLO TOWERS

I stayed in commercial development until 1990, when my father decided that he wanted in on the Las Vegas boom. The plan? To build the first high-rise timeshare property on the Strip. But there was a hitch: My father knew timeshare, but he didn't know building. So, even though my experience had been with commercial centers that went "out" instead of "up," he told me he wanted to bring me in as a partner. I was twenty-nine years old.

What would become Polo Towers—the first purposely built high-rise timeshare in the United States—conceived more than two hundred units when everyone else was building ten (twenty max). The deal required three lenders because at the time, no single lender was willing to take on that much financial risk. But the financing was my father's domain; I was in charge of building, designing, and operating the actual property, from concept to concrete. That meant every detail, from deciding how many floors the property would have to selecting the handles for every door and the decor for every room. I was operator, builder, supervisor, and interior decorator all in one. To me, an *entrepreneur* is an all-encompassing term rather than a title. It means you're in charge of—and accountable for—every detail, from every department.

If you've ever worked with family, you know there's no experience more stressful. We quibbled over numbers. Over design. Over timeline. Our personal and professional lives started to blur. This was no joyride. And so when Polo Towers opened its doors on December 29, 1992, it was an amazing moment and one I've treasured for my entire life. We had accomplished something great, and we had done it together.

My father's lenders relished the opening because the project itself came in on time and on budget, two things that rarely happen in the construction business.

## THE BEGINNING OF DIAMOND RESORTS

Four years later, my father sold his business to Starwood Capital. Rather than accept 3 percent of the proceeds as a partner payout, I instead got the untenable and unenviable task of being named "co-CEO" as my father bowed out. My counterpart was someone who had not previously dabbled in construction, real estate, or hospitality. We didn't know it then, but this co-led venture with two diametrically opposed leaders—one focused on spreadsheets and bottom lines and one (me) on people and the customer—was doomed from the very start.

At one point, my co-CEO made the decision to cut marketing by 30 percent to help save expenditures. I believed that while this would save on expenses, it would cost us dearly in profit and revenue. We disagreed about things, and eventually, it became obvious that it wouldn't be beneficial for the business to continue in its current form. I felt strongly that someone had to sell, and I felt just as strongly that it wasn't going to be me.

I believed in what we had built. I believed in the people running the day-to-day. I believed in the model that put the customer first—delivering exceptional service that didn't only meet expectations but exceeded them—would be a winning strategy.

Eventually, I was able to buy out all the partners, including my co-CEO. And that was the beginning of a new company, Worldstar Resorts: Diamond Resorts LLC.

Build a business model that puts the customer first, delivering exceptional service that doesn't only meet expectations but exceeds them.

To finance the operation, I took out a sixty-month loan from Textron, a lender that specifically worked in the timeshare space. Textron was astonished when I paid it back in three years and eight months—all from cash flow. I now owned 100 percent of my own company. And what a feeling it was.

In 2003, with the business established, Marriott came to me with a bid to buy the company that I couldn't turn down. By selling Marriott the physical property, but not the name of the company, the deal presented me with the financial luxury of being able to provide for my growing family while living comfortably for the rest of my life. But do you know what mattered most to me in all this? Hearing my father say, for what I believe to be the first time in my life, "You did good, son. I'm proud of you."

That was enough. Well, for a couple of years, anyway. But the entrepreneurial spirit doesn't "retire." It grows restless. It grows eager. It dreams of new possibilities and fresh starts.

I started looking for my next business endeavor.

## The Final Word

- There are no guarantees in what we do, only gambles.
- If only we'd be a little bit bolder, a little more aggressive, we could build more, do more, achieve more. Nothing meaningful was built without first risking something worthwhile.
- There will always be reasons *not* to start a company. The telltale sign of emerging entrepreneurs is not a once-in-a-generation idea or a perfected business plan but the confidence to bet on themselves.
- An entrepreneur is an all-encompassing identity, not a title. It means you're in charge of—and accountable for—every detail, from every department.

# The Sunterra Saga

S unterra. Ring any bells? There's a reason you haven't heard of it. It hasn't existed for more than ten years. Sunterra is the poster child of a "good business" undermined by bad values. The result here is the same as anywhere: The company crumbled under its own weight. Its demise involved fatal excesses, systemic dysfunction, scapegoating, and outright neglect. But what makes the story worth telling is not just what took it under but also the renewed principles, vision, and culture that gave it a second life as Diamond Resorts International.

This next section is an abridged account of the company's swift rise and rapid downfall. I tell it with full admission that I'm a biased historian— before acquiring Sunterra, I studied in full its operational mismanagement (the thought of which still makes my blood pressure rise). It's a complex, convoluted story to which there is little black and white and an abundance of gray. But if you're up for a challenge, I'll attempt to share Sunterra's track record with you, sparing no messy detail or unfortunate event, from a deeply personal conviction that you must know a company's past to appreciate its present and envision its future.

Here we go.

## Too Much, Too Quickly

Sunterra was founded in 1990, in the middle of the timeshare gold rush in the United States. A group of investors cobbled together nine properties under the distinctive name Signature Resorts. For the next ten years, the company grew and grew, buying up competitors as it sought to simultaneously expand its own owner base. The sky was the limit. It could do no wrong. The company went public only six short years later in 1996.

Over the course of one year, the company gobbled up resorts from Virginia to Hawaii, Florida to California, Arizona to Texas, England to Portugal. The destinations were exotic, but the debt required to underwrite the deals was exorbitant. By May 1998, the company, now officially Sunterra, operated eighty-five resorts in ten different countries, across multiple time zones. As if this weren't a sign that Sunterra had been undertaking too much, too quickly, it also resolved to operate Embassy Vacation Resorts and Westin Vacation Club.

Leadership realized that day-to-day operations were becoming unwieldy. And so, in a move that proved too little too late, it looked to consolidate its offices and move its people to a new corporate headquarters in Orlando, Florida, the epicenter of the timeshare industry.

This is where jaws usually hit the floor. The motivations were smart, but the execution was excessive. In the summer of 1999, Sunterra was in the process of locating new office space to house its six hundred central-Florida team members, plus an additional two hundred from other branches. It spent $3.7 million on an old Montgomery Ward store that had lain vacant for nearly seven years, and dedicated $22 million to the construction of a state-of-the-art corporate headquarters facility. Why not? Having reported sales of $352 million only the year before—second only to Marriott Vacation

Club International—the company's potential seemed limitless. Maybe it was. But leadership made shortsighted decisions looking to skim an extra buck in the here and now rather than plan for long-term growth.

Sunterra's profits plunged, and things only got worse from there. Its earnings were coming in below analyst expectations, and Sunterra leadership soon discovered $38 to $45 million in delinquent accounts in an in-depth review of company ledgers.

(The final number? A cool $43 million.)

So began a series of frantic moves that tried to right a ship, long after it had careened into a financial iceberg. A new CEO replaced the one hired only two years before. Then came the appointment of a co-CEO, president, and director of the company, in vain hopes to provide balance.

Sunterra's stock continued to drop until it ended a new fifty-two-week low with more than 6.4 million shares traded in a single day. The typical figure? Around 100,000 shares per day. That's more than sixty-four times the normal amount.

Imagine if the water you drank had sixty-four times the normal amount of impurities. If your heart beat sixty-four times more per minute than normal. If you were asked to lift more than sixty-four times your normal weight at the gym? If these analogies are extreme, it's because the reality of the situation was extreme. Sunterra was under incredible duress.

Shortly after, the company became the target of a high-profile class action lawsuit from investors who had purchased stock in the company.

## A Continued Downward Spiral

Things weren't exactly turning around. Plans for the cutting-edge new office space were put on ice. Having already invested $7 million in the new headquarters, Sunterra decided that the best course of action would be to sell the project to the county. The building originally designed to house more than eight hundred employees became a sheriff's office.

Although more attention and energy was poured into shoring up its dismal financial performance, Sunterra's downward spiral continued to gain momentum. In March 2000, Sunterra revealed it had lost nearly $60 million in the fourth quarter of 1999 alone. A new plan was set in motion: to "reorganize"—which was code for "pare back"—US operations, spin off certain assets, and slow construction on then-current projects. Perhaps this was sound judgment given the circumstances, but, as you'll see once again, it was terrible in execution.

Two months later, Sunterra confirmed it would be selling some of its resorts to keep the company from collapsing into financial ruin. However, it was absolutely silent about which of its properties would be up for sale.

Now, imagine you're one of Sunterra's three hundred thousand owners. You bought into the promise of having vacation for life—maybe with the idea that you'd be able to return to the same resort each and every time. That's where you'd make friends. That's where you'd find your favorite ice cream shop or burger joint to take your family. That's where you'd make memories. Or, maybe you purchased into the Sunterra vision with dreams of traveling the world and sampling all the properties under the Sunterra umbrella. Now, imagine that this dream—whether to return to a familiar place year after year or to travel the globe—is dashed because the properties once offered directly to you may no longer be available to anyone.

> Transparency. Accountability. Communication. They become *more* important in times of crisis, not less.

It wasn't just poor decision making that led to this point; it was the lack of communication, credibility, and certainty that owners were being asked to cope with as they tried to make plans for the future. Transparency. Accountability. Communication. They become *more* important in times of crisis, not less.

It's no exaggeration to say that each passing day seemed to bring more bad news for the hobbled company. In the first quarter of 2000, Sunterra posted a loss of $16 million, in addition to admitting it was having real difficulty paying back its creditors. In fact, the company missed a scheduled $6.5 million payment to one lender and defaulted on a $4 million bank loan.

If the writing wasn't on the wall before, by now it was etched in stone.

## Borrowed Money, Borrowed Time

What became blindingly apparent to investors, owners, and even casual stock market observers was how unsustainably dependent Sunterra was on borrowed money. The company's revenue in 1999 had been over $500 million, but its debt at the end of that same year was $682 million. By the end of March 2000, its debt had ballooned to *$711* million.

Credit may have been cheap for Sunterra, but it wasn't free. When the company finally realized there simply wasn't a sufficient bloodstream of cash running through the business to keep operations afloat, it was already taking on water.

In May 2000, Sunterra announced that it would eliminate 930 jobs (more than its could-have-been Florida headquarters was designed to accommodate) from its 7,800 team members. But eliminating 12 percent of its workforce wasn't enough to create the liquidity needed to buoy its operations (though it was certainly enough to fracture company morale, create an aura of distrust and suspicion, and undermine the guest experience as a result).

The company looked for scapegoats wherever it could find them: restructuring expenses, higher market costs, weak bookings, bad press. Realistically, there were deeper structural problems that had become so embedded in the fabric of the company that its leadership had difficulty discerning them.

Sunterra filed for Chapter 11 bankruptcy protection on May 31, 2000, carrying $850 million in debt and $1 billion in assets.

I'd like to say it came as a shock, but...

The New York Stock Exchange halted trading the stock. Trading never resumed; the stock was ultimately delisted from the exchange entirely.

Without a moment's hesitation, the company's credit rating fell from CCC to DD.

## LOOKING FOR HELP IN LEADERS

While Sunterra was scrambling to find its footing and set any sort of financial order, it decided once again that new leadership was needed. It found its man in Gregory Rayburn, a corporate turnaround whisperer at the firm Jay Alix and Associates, now AlixPartners.

Rayburn saw a company at odds with its own potential. The timeshare industry as a whole was seeing solid performance across the board. So why shouldn't Sunterra be able to attract new customers? It had the right pieces. It had the right properties. It had the right framework to succeed. Rayburn recognized that other companies didn't have the same range and diversity of resorts that Sunterra had.

He was right. But what he didn't factor in, and what the company never accounted for, was the right internal culture. And as we'll see, culture—not strategy—is what makes or breaks companies of all sizes, in all industries, in all lines of business. (You learn more about a company from studying its culture than its strategy.)

And with Sunterra's millions of outstanding shares trading on over-the-counter pink sheets—a quote service notorious for basement prices on risky stocks—it was merely a matter of time before the creditors took control. Rayburn may have had all the right pieces, but he couldn't animate them because he couldn't reset employee morale, attitude, and outlook.

> You learn more about a company from studying its culture than its strategy.

It was *in spite* of having all the right pieces and precisely *because* it lacked the right people that Sunterra's situation became so fraught. What's more, this one company spooked the markets to such an extent that it threatened to destabilize an entire industry. More lenders, in more places, were becoming hesitant to lend to *any* timeshare company, fearing Sunterra wasn't just a cautionary tale but a harbinger for the industry.

In November 2001, Nicholas Benson, formerly of Sunterra Europe, became the company's umpteenth CEO. He had no illusions about the job or the company. But he hoped for a clean start.

That's not exactly what he got.

## THE BLAME GAME

In early 2002, Sunterra announced plans to relocate its US operations to Las Vegas. By that time, the company was already operating two separate divisions, one in Florida (not in a new office) and the other in Europe. It quickly became apparent that the left hand didn't know what the right hand was doing. And so, the company lashed out: It blamed someone else.

Sunterra filed a lawsuit against its accounting firm, Arthur Andersen of Enron infamy, for merely purporting to audit the company's financial statements for 1998 and 1999. The argument? That Arthur Andersen should have discerned that Sunterra's financial condition was materially overstated and conveyed a false impression of financial well-being.[1]

Sunterra emerged from bankruptcy protection on July 30, 2002. Unbelievable as it may seem, the resuscitated company's first move was to borrow an exorbitant $300 million from Merrill Lynch Mortgage Capital Inc. The plan was to pay off $160 million in loans and continue growing the business. For the next three years, the focus was on nursing the brand back to fiscal health and rehabilitating its badly blemished public image. The company got a break in 2005 when its stock was listed on the NASDAQ trading market, ending a four-year market embargo. But financial performance was mixed, at best. In March 2004, Sunterra had not only posted a loss for the fourth quarter of 2002 but also for the entire year. However, it announced that revenue from its vacation interests had risen 17 percent in 2003, and overall earnings before taxes and charges had grown 80 percent. This crossbred track record left investors and owners (and senior leadership, too) scratching their heads.

## THE NEED FOR A CUSTOMER-SERVICE MIND-SET

In 2004, the company infused itself with new energy by changing all three independent members of its board of directors, which was no small move. And in came three highly accomplished and highly intelligent professionals: James Dickerson, Olof Nelson, and James Weissenborn. (As an objective corporate historian, if it weren't for Weissenborn's incredible financial acumen and strong corporate background, Sunterra would have gone bankrupt *again*. Weissenborn bears much of the credit for flying a wounded plane back to base.)

But the board of directors misstepped by placing its laser focus on preserving stockholder equity, not on building long-term value. That's because none of these new additions to the board of directors happened to have a hospitality background. Focusing on financial performance in the short term, without a long-view strategy, meant perpetually stumbling from one crisis into the next.

It should come as no surprise that Sunterra's earnings trajectory continued in a way that can only be described as a roller-coaster ride. The company was quick to buy properties that it hoped would stabilize its cash flow—but the goal was to buy more, not buy smarter. Rather than obsessing over the customer experience and customer satisfaction, leadership seemed to want to more strictly follow the revenue numbers and percentage growth, not recognizing the direct, undeniable, causal effect that *quality* has on *performance*.

In an interview with the *Las Vegas Review-Journal* in 2004, then-CEO Nick Benson was asked what his primary focus was, given the myriad challenges still facing the troubled and humbled company. He replied that the team was ambitious to be the global leader in the industry, by any metric.

There was nothing wrong with what he said. But the words were generic, with no personalization, individualization, or keen sense of purpose. You could apply them to nearly any enterprise—perhaps a widgets factory or a fruit conglomerate—and the reader would be none the wiser. Where was the passion for delivering exceptional vacation experiences? Where was the priority of connecting a team to a culture of hospitality? Where was the example of service leadership? In my opinion, it was missing.

## CONTINUED TROUBLES

Shuffling money around worked—for a while. Sunterra's third-quarter revenues in 2004 grew by nearly 50 percent while its profits more than doubled. The biggest part of that success stemmed from the company's Hawaii properties, which drove substantial profits (despite an active hurricane season that year). The company's European operations were also firing up, generating nearly $4 million in profit over that same period.

But it didn't last. By the second quarter of 2005, Sunterra again posted a quarterly loss, this time approximately $50 million. Once again, the company tried to buy its way into profitability, purchasing the Misiones del Cabo Hotel and Resort in Cabo San Lucas, Mexico. Another move it made was to purchase the website of a failed cruise agency to tap into a different customer base. Later, when I learned this, I thought of a saying that Albert Einstein is often credited with: "The definition of insanity is doing the same thing over and over again but expecting different results."

As 2005 was coming to a close, Sunterra reported yet another quarterly loss. The company's continued lack of focus and erratic business strategy was feeding investor fears that Sunterra was miles away from turning any sort of predictable, stable returns. From investors to owners to employees, everyone was on edge. With good reason.

In April 2006, a former Sunterra team member alleged that the company had engaged in several accounting misdeeds in its European operations, primarily in Spain. The man emailed Sunterra's new auditor, Grant Thornton, in March, outlining his concerns and providing a copy of a similar email sent to the company in December 2005.

To Sunterra's credit, the board ordered an immediate investigation, following the evidence wherever it led. The board was determined to discover which of the allegations, if any, were true, which were false, and who was accountable.

In time, the board placed Nick Benson on paid administrative leave and tapped James Weissenborn to become Sunterra's interim CEO. It wasn't an easy decision for Weissenborn; in fact, he tried to turn it down multiple times. But Weissenborn, to his credit, took on the challenge.

While I've attempted to keep track of CEOs in this retelling, I can't begin to account for the churn throughout company ranks. From the executive level to front-of-house staff, the best people were fleeing in droves. It's hard for me to think of these good people who felt like they needed to leave their jobs.

## LOOKING FOR A BUYER

Barely a week after the announcement that Benson would be stepping down as CEO, one of Sunterra's major shareholders began vocally and relentlessly demanding the sale of the company, along with its entire European division. Robert Chapman, then a managing member of Chapman Capital, filed a Schedule 13D with the US Securities and Exchange Commission (SEC) to explore a full-scale auction.

He had good reason to be upset, given the company's substandard performance, its sinking financials, and unsettled accounting practices. At the time, Chapman owned approximately 1.6 million shares of Sunterra, and he believed he knew who was responsible for his losses. The target of his frustration? The European division, which he called "a malignant cancer ulcerating at Sunterra's healthy North America division."[2] The colorful language continued in a letter, dated June 28, 2006, to Sunterra's chairman, David Gubbay: "Chapman Capital believes that Sunterra's Board of Directors has treated their fiduciary duty of due care worse than they would a timeshare in a construction site Porta-Potti."[3]

It seems Chapman's distinctive choice of imagery made an impact. Two weeks after he sounded his clarion call to sell the company, Sunterra announced it would hire an investment banker to explore long-term alternatives for the company, including the possibility of selling outright.[4] It was clear that big changes were afoot, but no one knew exactly how big these changes would be or how quickly they would come.

On July 7, Sunterra was delisted again—this time from the NASDAQ stock exchange—over concerns about the company's investigation of its European accounting operations. Less than a month later, on July 26, Nick Benson left the company and was asked to resign his post on Sunterra's board of directors.[5]

In a swift move, Sunterra appointed John Ziegelman of CD Capital Management. Not only was Ziegelman a longtime proponent of selling Sunterra, but also his company controlled nearly 7 percent of Sunterra stock. Naturally, he pushed his keen interest in selling the company—fast, and for more than it was worth. Only, Ziegelman's goal was complicated by a Sunterra announcement that it would reinstate its financial results for the past three years, due to the underpayment of taxes at its Spanish properties.

If the goal was to find a serious buyer, time was running out.

The downward spiral was officially out of control. In September 2006, Sunterra cut the compensation of its CEO, demoted its COO, and put the whole of its European operations up for sale. What's more, confidential conversations were leaking out of the Las Vegas headquarters faster than water draining through a sieve. This made vitally important strategic decisions all the more difficult.

After a clear-eyed look at who could possibly be the mole, Weissenborn concluded that the Las Vegas headquarters had been bugged. He moved company conversations from the CEO's office to janitorial spaces to prevent any potential extortionists, hawk opportunists, or adversaries from listening in.

Still, that wasn't enough. Management had grave concerns about radio intercepts, and about being followed. Business spies were so relentless, even family members of Sunterra officers became targets. Leaders suffered through twenty-hour days accompanied by ceaseless stress, suspicion, and paranoia.[6]

Then, the lawsuits came pouring in. Three investors' suits alleged Sunterra had "filed misleading financial results from 2002 to 2005, and that the value of its stock was severely impacted as a result."[7] By the year's end, Sunterra spent more than $12 million on investigations, external consultants and experts, and operational reviews—all before sending a single penny to European tax authorities.

Come 2007, Sunterra completed its analysis of the unpaid tax situation in Spain. The company had originally estimated the figure to be in the ballpark of $4 million. Try more than *tripling* that sum. The final tab came to nearly $14 million in unpaid withholding taxes, income taxes, values-added taxes, interest, and surcharges.

If the numbers are hard to follow, picture this. Sunterra was up to its neck in financial quicksand. If something didn't happen—and soon—the company's remaining shareholders risked losing their investments, the company's remaining five thousand team members risked losing their jobs, and more than three hundred thousand owners from around the world risked losing their vacation deeds, their pieces of happiness and relaxation, their peace of mind.

### The Final Word

- Transparency, accountability, and communication become *more* important in times of crisis, not less.
- You can learn more about a company from studying its culture than its tactics.
- Only a long-view strategy can build something of long-term value.
- Be the role model you want for yourself.

# Toward a Turnaround

I did warn you that the Sunterra story was not for the faint of heart.

From the whiplash-inducing leadership changes, to the needless hemorrhaging of company dollars, to the questionable ethics and actions that had become commonplace until the very point of bringing the former industry wunderkind to its knees, the only constant in this narrative is the near total disregard for the company's owners: the everyday guests it was meant to be serving.

No one deserves to be treated this way.

What the company needed was a person who had "grown up" in the industry; had built successful vacation-ownership properties; and knew the dedication, attention to detail, and diligence that went into running them. Sunterra needed someone who could make customer satisfaction the company's paramount priority, someone who could implement a plan that would, in time, fix the company's finances.

Frankly, a few years into my "early retirement" after selling my company to Marriott, I was restless. I needed the challenge of Sunterra—knowing that both employees and guests would be counting on me—to re-energize me, give me purpose, and make me feel like I had something more to contribute.

It was an improbable match, but the more I learned about Sunterra, the more I saw untapped potential both in the company and in myself. There were jobs, investments, and, yes, there was opportunity at stake. I began to ask myself, "What if?"

What if I took a bet on myself and leveraged my experience with Polo Towers—admittedly only a single property, not a portfolio of several dozen, let alone nearly one hundred—and tried to resuscitate Sunterra? I could keep the company largely intact, whereas other investors were looking to tear it into piecemeal components, stripping off parts like it was an old car abandoned in a junkyard. What if I poured my energies into learning Sunterra from the ground up—not just examining its books but also visiting its properties, talking to owners and guests, holding listening sessions with its team members? As an outsider, maybe I could audit the company's cultural and performance woes to get to the bottom of what really went wrong.

At first, James Weissenborn didn't believe he had a serious buyer to consider. Yes, there were many people making calls, but they were mostly people looking for spin-offs and subvalue deals. I wanted a fair shot at turning this company around, so I was willing to offer a fair price. But first, I'd have to fully understand the situation.

One ironclad confidentiality agreement later, I was in.

## Doing My Research

After barely scratching the company's surface, I saw why so many would-be buyers were scared away. Consider the following:

- Sunterra's US operations were on a September fiscal cycle, while the entire European entity was on a December fiscal cycle.

- Two totally separate sets of books scrambled the company's accounting records. There were even two different operating systems: a version of Oracle in the United States and a second version in Europe.

- An array of reservation systems—none of which integrated with the next—made booking resorts globally a nightmare not only for team members but for guests as well.

By and large, the company was operationally, culturally, and administratively split down the Atlantic Ocean, with nothing but common ownership in name uniting the business as a whole.

> It's easy to see problems in business, but it takes a
> trained eye to see opportunities.

These issues notwithstanding, here's what I still knew to be true: Sunterra had a customer base of over three hundred thousand customers worldwide, with resorts in the most desirable locations on earth. Had these customers been treated the way they should be? No. Had these properties been kept up properly? No. Did this erode the innate value in both? *Not a chance.*

It's easy to see problems in business, but it takes a trained eye to see opportunities. With the right care, leadership, and hard work, we could nurse the properties back to gleaming allure and treat the customers the way they always deserved to be treated. This was the underlying value that Sunterra's old guard neglected for the sake of boosting margins, chasing incremental financial gains, and cutting costs by cutting corners.

I believed we could do something greater.

## Seeing the Untapped Potential

I have many mentors in my life and many more people in business, even if I haven't yet had the chance to meet them, whose work I've studied, learned from, and greatly admire. Lynda Resnick, in particular, is a leader whose work I've highly regarded from afar.

Resnick and her husband, Stewart, are business moguls in California. They have an uncanny knack for identifying and seizing opportunities at precisely the right moment. But where some might attribute their success to luck—being in the right place at the right time and making a lucky bet—I attribute it to their keen ability to uncover innate value where others can only spot surface-level convention.

In her book, *Rubies in the Orchard*, Resnick describes the surreal experience of sitting around a conference table, listening to a hoard of consultants tell her husband what he should do with his recently acquired pomegranate orchard. The consensus? Since Americans weren't familiar with the fruit, the best course of action would be to sell their wonderfully vibrant, deep, and merlot-like juice as fillers. If they added the pomegranate juice to other fruit cocktails, Americans would be none the wiser.

> **None of them had considered the untapped potential of what it could become. None of them saw the *value* that Stewart's pomegranate orchard had to offer.**

It took all of Resnick's restraint not to boot the consultants—so pleased with their two-by-twos, numeric projections, and Venn diagrams—out of the room. None of them had spent the time getting to know her product. None of them had considered the untapped potential of what it could become. None of them saw the *value* that Stewart's pomegranate orchard had to offer.

Resnick knew better. She took over her husband's pomegranate business. And no, the pomegranates wouldn't be yet another filler in one more sugary sweet syrup juice, replete with artificial flavors and deficient in natural ones. Instead, Resnick would make pomegranates the star of the show, introducing the American public to a fruit, natural juice, and product that they had limited, *if any*, exposure to before.

She commissioned studies on the benefits of the fruit. She spent hours creating, refining, and editing marketing plans that highlighted the pomegranate's natural properties. Hers would be an honest campaign. And soon, she launched a new product: POM Wonderful.[1] You may know it from its crazy creative advertising. You may know it for its incredible health benefits. You may even drink it regularly yourself. Today, thousands of Americans do.

All of which is to say, despite all the overgrown weeds—the corporate mismanagement, the botched priorities of financial performance over customer service, the confusing and complicated operating system—I knew Sunterra had its own "rubies in the orchard." I intended to help them grow.

But to fix the company, I'd have to own it first.

## Making Our Offer

Not surprisingly, purchasing a company that doesn't have accurate financial statements—at least three years' worth compromised, in fact—is a laborious and painfully time-consuming process. My team and I would have to work hand in hand with the SEC to ensure every step was aboveboard. Continuing in this spirit of full disclosure, we would have to reveal to Sunterra's board of directors that, quite frankly, we didn't know what the SEC would approve and what it would reject. It was a time of mutual good faith, working toward an agreement that both sides would consider a win-win.

> If you're not willing to bet boldly on your work, question how confident you really are.

On our side, we equipped ourselves with a small battalion of lawyers, accountants, and business professionals to conduct our own independent

review of Sunterra. We scrubbed all the numbers, visited all the properties—
and I mean *all* the properties—with a view of composing an accurate financial
model of the company. It was an unheard-of mission to create a financial model
and cash flow capabilities against all but nonexistent financial statements,
which took over six months to complete. But in the end, our efforts were so
exhaustive, so detail oriented, that I personally signed a representation war-
ranty attesting that our estimation's accuracy surpassed 95 percent accuracy of
the real number Sunterra was worth, a figure that could only be pinned down
precisely after the deal was closed in a full audit. To give our lenders even more
assurance in the quality of our work, I agreed that for *every* dollar we missed
outside of our 95 percent projection, we'd insert an *additional* dollar of equity
into the transaction. I believe that if you're not willing to bet boldly on your
work, you may need to question how confident you really are.

We had submitted our best and final offer. Now, we just had to wait
and see.

## The Purchase

In March 2007, the news was out. "Diamond Resorts says it will tender a
bid to purchase Sunterra Corp. for about $700 million," read the *Orlando
Business Journal* on March 12. We had purchased Sunterra's stock at a 35
percent premium over the closing price just a few days prior.[2]

Fair price, fair offer.

### PUTTING PEOPLE FIRST

I had no secrets about my intentions for the company. I made my plan clear
then, just as I do now: We'd concentrate on getting the company in good
financial health, not at the expense of good customer service but by raising
our standards and prioritizing the guest experience. From the purchase day
forward, we would be about putting people—not profits—first. I was confident the latter would follow the former.

At first, when reporters from financial newspapers and journals came calling, they were frustrated by my response. They wanted to talk spreadsheets; I talked bed sheets—we'd be updating the bedding, installing flat-screen TVs, purchasing new furniture, creating a more robust list of activities for children, and the list went on. I insisted that as the new CEO, my tenure wouldn't simply be another changing of the guard. There was a new governing order in power, one that cared about its guests and team members above all.

Diamond Resorts would be about putting people—not profits—first.

That's why I made it doubly clear to resort staff that their work lives were going to change, too. No, not because I was cleaning house—I knew the team members, their institutional knowledge, and their camaraderie with regular guests was one of the strongest assets we had. No, their lives were going to change because they'd be given the license to actually make a difference at work. No more bureaucracy. No more stifled communication. We would teach what hospitality meant, what the Meaning of Yes symbolized, and then trust our people to carry out this vision in their own way, with their own vigor, and with our full support.

## RAISING THE STAKES

About one month later, in April 2007, we completed the acquisition. By purchasing Sunterra, Diamond Resorts International became one of the industry's biggest players overnight. In size, if not in reputation, we rivaled the likes of Wyndham and Marriott vacation-ownership programs. We always took our work seriously. We owned our responsibility to our people. But now, we raised the stakes to another level.

We, the executive staff, poured ourselves into not just developing a growth strategy but also delivering a sorely needed shot in the arm. We prioritized property modernization and attention to detail: exactly what was needed to generate organic excitement, satisfy returning visitors, and—with any luck, and in time—jump-start new sales. But we wouldn't stop there. We'd also pursue untapped opportunities in the Middle East, Mexico, and Asia. There was no corner of the earth we wouldn't go to for our customers (which led to one particularly interesting escapade I'll dive into later), because we were committed to ensuring they had every vacation opportunity at their fingertips—whether that meant safari adventure or beachside escape, city living or country relaxation.

> **Every decision we'd make, every action we'd take, would be oriented by a deep understanding of who our customers were, what they wanted, and how we couldn't just meet— but needed to exceed—their expectations.**

Revamping team members' expectations. Improving our current properties. Setting our sights on new destinations. Admittedly, it was a lot to take on, especially when Diamond Resorts leadership members were just finding their post-Sunterra sea legs. What made this multipronged strategy possible—which, under other circumstances, could have dissolved into chaos— was having a North Star. Every decision we'd make, every action we'd take, would be oriented by a deep understanding of who our customers were, what they wanted, and how we couldn't just meet—but needed to exceed—all their expectations.

How does this work? Through the principles of hospitality.

## The Final Word

- It's easy to see problems in business, but it takes a trained eye to see opportunities. Consider the untapped potential of what something can become; see the value in what something has to offer.

- If you're not willing to bet boldly on your work, question how confident you really are in what you're doing. Better to go back to the drawing board earlier rather than later.

- Putting people over profits is the first step to ensuring you have a team that cares about the company's bottom line as much as you do. Invest in your team members and employees; they're the greatest assets you have.

- Let every decision you make and action you take be oriented by a deep understanding of who your customers are.

- Why meet customer expectations, when you can aspire to exceed them?

# PART TWO

# Focus Unrelentingly
# on the Guest

# The Meaning of Yes

It's one thing to build a reputation from scratch; it's another to collect the shards of a broken image, rebuild trust, and earn back credibility after it's been lost.

Sunterra owners didn't know me, and I didn't know them (at least not well enough). But from the start, I knew what they deserved: a five-star vacation experience without the five-star price tags; team members who knew them by name and genuinely cared about their stay, going out of their way to make it as enjoyable as possible; and leadership who didn't just listen to but learned from the customers themselves.

Although I knew I had my work cut out for me, I was determined to do what was necessary to change things for the better. Over time, I developed a way of thinking and doing business, which, in the context of everything, seemed radical to others but essential to me. It had everything to do with the way we approach people and understand hospitality, and since then, I've come to see that it applies to almost any situation, no matter the industry. I'll show you how I arrived at the Meaning of Yes in the pages that follow, but first let me introduce you to the concept:

> The Meaning of Yes is a business's North Star, a company's directional compass. It's about doing what's right for the guest in the moment to the best of our ability—regardless of precedent or minutiae-riddled policy. It's about meeting needs and exceeding expectations, being 100 percent committed to the customer experience, and trusting that your guests, your clients, and your customers can help you decide where your organization needs to go.

When you live the Meaning of Yes, you establish a culture that people want to be a part of, set positive expectations for those around you, and create an experience that puts people first. No other concept has made a greater impact in my work over the years.

## Focus on the Customers

As the new CEO and founder of Diamond Resorts International, I started out by reading a Boston Consulting Group report the previous management had commissioned on the state of our business. If you've heard anything about Boston Consulting Group, you know it's one of the most exclusive, sought-after, prestigious management consulting firms on the planet. It has served Fortune 500 companies for decades and sourced top-tier talent from Ivy League colleges for even longer. But when I read this $5 million report, I discovered jargon, not understanding; and information, not insight. It was full of numbers, figures, and charts that in coded form tried to explain what the old business should become *strictly in terms of percentages and timelines.* Worst of all, it focused on the competition, not on our customers.

Where were the sections on our people, our talent? Where was the imperative to reconnect with our guests, our raisons d'être? If it was anywhere at all in this supposedly sterling report, it was so buried between the pie graphs and infographics that I couldn't see it.

I was furious. This was exactly the sort of ivory-tower leadership that had caused Sunterra to fall out of touch with its owners and investors in the first place.

So, I took that $5 million report and did what anyone would do. I threw it in the trash, where it belonged.

## Spend your time obsessing over your customers, not over your competition.

If I wanted to reconnect with the heart of what was now Diamond Resorts, I couldn't be locked away in an office. I had to be present where our business mattered most: at the check-in desks, activity centers, poolsides, and housekeeping carts. I had to get out of headquarters and get on-site.

I anticipated that the next year would be the most exhausting of my life. I was right. I was away from my small children more than any dad should be, visiting our network of properties. When I was talking to families sitting around the fireplace in New England, I thought of my own back home, missing me like I missed them. What kept me going was knowing that my work, my being present with our customers, if not my family, would make a difference to thousands of families in some of the most precious moments of their lives: while they were on vacation.

## NOTICE THE DETAILS

I was a one-man qualitative research machine. I became obsessed with stories from the people I met. I tried my best to ask about every little detail of their experience, good and bad, so I could better understand this person's perspective and where they were coming from. I began keeping a list, what I called my golden nuggets of ideas I learned from my guests that we could implement not just resort-wide, but company-wide.

These may sound like small details, but on the whole, they make up the entire guest experience: soft, high-quality towels that wrap around you instead of those that barely tie around your waist; valets that greet you with a smile upon arrival and direct you toward the front desk so you aren't left wondering which way to turn after an exhausting plane ride; a clear and organized area behind the front desk so guests feel confident that you have their full attention and can accommodate their specific requests.

Already, our guests were teaching me more than a static, old-school consulting analysis ever could. No matter what business you're in, remember what Amazon CEO Jeff Bezos once said: "If we can keep our competitors focused on us while we stay focused on the customer, ultimately we'll turn out all right."[1]

At that point, even after twenty-five years in hospitality, I was being challenged by my guests to rethink the basics. And that got me to wondering: What were other details I could improve, if only I thought to take another look at the status quo?

I'll give you four easy examples that I hope demonstrate Diamond's commitment to ensuring the highest standard across every aspect of the guest experience from check-in to checkout was the best it possibly could be.

1. **The kids' menu.** When hospitality wonks think of restaurants, we typically consider the wine list, the quality and inventiveness of the menu, the service of the host and front-of-house staff. Who does this leave out? The kids! Think of it: You're on a family vacation, and part of the joy of being a parent or grandparent is taking this time for everyone to enjoy one another's company, together. But if the restaurant offerings are only catered to the adults, are the little ones really getting the experience they deserve?

So I called in the experts: my kids.

We traveled to the Ka'anapali Beach Club resort on Maui's western shores, and after a few hours of splashing in the pool and playing on the beach, I called Kevin, Jacob, Jaden, and Tatiana over. I needed their help. Their job was to taste test the kids' menu and to give the chefs their honest, unfiltered, and constructive feedback.

---

**Our commitment to guests is best judged by how we treat our youngest patrons, not just those who pay the bills.**

---

The chicken fingers should have less breading, more white meat; the grilled cheese could be "gooey-ier"; the ice cream sundaes should have more whipped cream and chocolate sauce (but hold the cherry on top). The chefs took note, and the kids gave praise: The Shirley Temples were just right, and on the breakfast menu, the scrambled eggs were the fluffiest they ever had.

All work should be this fun.

Could we have gotten away without this exercise? Sure. But is making sure mealtime is something the whole family looks forward to part of delivering an amazing guest experience? Absolutely. Parents with particularly picky eaters could breathe a little easier, knowing their kids would make dinner a time for conversation and laughter instead of a battle. Perfecting the kids' menu enhances the vacation in myriad intangible ways. And I believe that our commitment to guests is best judged by how we treat our youngest patrons, not just those who pay the bills.

**2. The pillows.** I had been on the road for weeks, introducing myself to different team members at different resorts, when finally, I had the opportunity to spend a few nights at home, in my own bed. I remember the first night—lying down, exhausted, all too eager to close my eyes. How good resting my head on my pillow felt.

I jolted upright. This feeling right here, right now, should be the feeling that all my guests experience when they come to one of our properties—be it for a day, a week, a month. Pure relaxation. Pure comfort. Pure peace of mind.

## When it comes to cost, obsess over value, not price.

I called my executive team and asked them to ensure that for thirty days, I slept on a different pillow every night (cue princess and the pea jokes here). I compared our pillows to standard industry options; to top-of-the-line options; and to allergenic, thermo-controlled, who-knew-a-pillow-was-supposed-to-do-that options.

Today, Diamond Resorts International uses only Sobel Westex pillows—because they're the best. They're more expensive, but because they're top quality, they last longer and provide our guests with the experience they're meant to enjoy in the first place. We cared about delivering real value to our guests, not the up-front cost, and it made all the difference. (In fact, when a well-intentioned team member came to me years later, suggesting we could save money by switching to a less expensive but similar model, I had him bring me one of our pillows and one of the competitor's. Right then and there, in my office, I took my letter opener and sliced each one right down the middle. The Sobel Westex pillow had extra layers of cushion; the competitor's did not. Needless to say, we stayed with the costlier option.) When it comes to cost, obsess over value, not price.

**3. The aesthetics.** I was visiting one of our properties in Scottsdale, Arizona, to check on the progress of our landscaping. I had been there a few weeks prior and was underwhelmed to say the least by the lack of desert greenery that lined the roadway up to the front entrance.

In any business, first impressions are critical. If you're a storefront, you want signage that not only catches attention but also holds it. If you're an e-commerce business, you want a website layout that is clean, bold, and intuitive to navigate. And if you're a resort, you want an entrance, a gateway, a front door that immediately communicates to visitors, "You've arrived, and we can't wait to take care of you."

That's not exactly the impression cast by withering plants in a dusty landscape.

---

**Putting care into how things look creates an overall feeling and impression for guests and demonstrates to them that they matter.**

---

The resort management explained that they had submitted the budget allocation request to corporate *more than fifteen months ago* and still hadn't received an answer one way or the other. They were taken aback when I told them that corporate, a hundred odd miles away, would no longer be approving these sorts of spend asks. The people on-site knew what the property needed more than headquarters, so go get it done.

When I returned, I was blown away by the beauty of the resort's prickly pear, blooming desert roses, and ripe yellow fruit growing on barrel cacti contrasted against the red soil. It looked like something straight out of a Hollywood movie. And that's exactly how I wanted my guests to feel. Putting care into how things look creates an overall feeling and impression for guests and demonstrates to them that they matter.

**4. The things people don't always notice.** I spent the night at the same property in Scottsdale to talk to management about the general improvements and plans for even more upgrades to the grounds. The next morning, as I was getting ready to depart, I dropped my watch off my bedside table. I knelt down to pick it up, peered under the bed, and found my watch . . . right next to a humongous ball of lint.

How many other guests had checked under the bed for missing items—a lost sock, an earring, a child's toy—and had the same experience? The thought of it made me cringe. And then it made me determined never to let that happen to another guest, ever again.

---

## True hospitality is caring for the details that perhaps no one else will notice.

---

I called an emergency meeting with the housekeeping staff. I explained that it's not just big-ticket items that everyone knows to look for that count—the linens, the bathroom, the minibar—but the little things that, yes, some guests might not appreciate, but you will.

I showed the staff how to tuck the corners of the bedding in tightly, how to fluff the pillows, how to clean the blinds, how to restock toiletries. And then, I got down on my knees and showed them the difference it made by cleaning under the beds, chairs, and other pieces of furniture in the room.

Now, when a guest looks under the bed for a dropped watch or missing item, what do they find? A small sign that affirms, "Yes, we clean under here, too." True hospitality is caring for the details that perhaps no one else will notice.

From guaranteeing our guests had top-of-the-line amenities to ensuring no detail was too small to overlook, these were first-order changes that transformed Sunterra properties into Diamond Resorts. And many hoteliers would have stopped there, patted themselves on the back, and considered it a turnaround job well done. But I wanted to go further. I wanted to let all my guests know that I was committed to taking their priorities and making them a reality. I knew my focus needed to be unrelentingly on my guests.

This is how a Meaning of Yes culture is created. And it's how you change a legacy.

## The Final Word

- Don't focus on your competition; focus on your customers.

- It's important not to always be locked away in an office; make sure to be present, where business matters the most, whether that's the factory floor, the sales center, or with guests.

- Listen to—and learn from—your customers. The guests aren't always right—but they always have something to teach you.

- When it comes to cost, obsess over value, not price.

- True hospitality is caring for the details others will miss. Hospitality is about making yourself proud and others comfortable.

# Be My Guest

I had started the important work of focusing on the needs and perspectives of my guests at Diamond properties. But I quickly realized what a daunting task it was and that it was clearly something that was easier said than done. How do you get the constructive opinions of three hundred thousand people who span the globe?

If you're me, you admit you're out of your depth and ask for help.

I turned to my friend Frank Luntz to help me better understand what guests wanted most of all and how they would most appreciate us delivering that value to them. For those of you who haven't seen Frank on *60 Minutes*, CBS News, or Fox; watched him host televised pre-election focus groups to get a pulse on voter priorities, concerns, and hopes; or read his editorials in *The Times* (London), *The New York Times*, and *U.S. News & World Report*, suffice it to say he is one of the most respected researchers and communications professionals in America today. To put it bluntly, President Barack

Obama once said, "When Frank Luntz invites you to talk to his focus group, you talk to his focus group."[1]

Frank's spent a career understanding people—what makes them tick, what motivates them, what spurs behavioral changes. He's developed proprietary methodologies designed to isolate the very arguments, appeals, and facts (what he calls "words that work") that cause people to pay attention and take notice. But best of all, Frank has an uncanny and inimitable knack for relating to people, getting them to open up about what they really feel and why.

He was my guy.

Together, we set out to earn a deeper understanding of our guest. Not just their profile: age, demographics, vacation habits. That's the easy stuff. No, we set out to understand the emotional undercurrents that went into planning a vacation. I wanted to be true to my promise of putting guests first. For me, a relentless focus on the guest meant not just listening to their feedback and collecting some stats, but understanding what they hoped for in a vacation, what felt meaningful to them in the experience, and what they wanted to carry with them when they went home.

## What Guests Want

In 2007, we began surveying our guests in the United States and the United Kingdom. Across geographies and life stages, three key themes consistently rose to the top:

1. simplicity

2. choice

3. comfort

What we repeatedly heard our guests telling us was that an ideal vacation consists of a hassle-free experience that encourages relaxation and flexibility;

in essence, it affords guests the license to do precisely what they want to do, when they want to do it, and on their own terms.

We probed deeper. Of our owners worldwide, only 13 percent were under the age of forty, while almost a full third of our owners said they were sixty years old or older. The household income was well above the national average but consisted of many two-income families. That meant at home, our guests had to budget not only their expenditures but also their time. More than half of our members characterized the ideal vacation as "a place to relax" instead of other possible choices, such as "a place with activities I like" or "excitement." When we asked for their number one reason they chose to purchase a vacation property with us in the first place, "quality" rose to the top with a wide berth, followed only by "saving money" and "flexibility."

> ## Customers want you to succeed, and they'll help you do so—but only if you have the courage to include them in your decision-making processes.

When it came to the properties themselves, we were astonished that customers identified the quality and experience of their rooms as being of primary importance. The rooms even overtook the quality and details of a property's location, dining options, and resort amenities. It makes sense when you think about it—whether you're on a beach excursion or city tour, you always come back to your room. If that's not comfortable, your vacation isn't comfortable, full stop.

Through this, I began to see that customers want you to succeed and they'll even help you do so, but only if you have the courage to include them in your decision-making process. Was it difficult to collect, analyze, and implement all this feedback? Yes. Was it worth it? Absolutely. It changed the course of Diamond's history.

## Above all else, Rooms should be **WELCOMING**

Other than comfortable, which do you want MOST
in a hotel room or timeshare unit? (Combined)

| TOTAL | MEMBERS | OWNERS | |
|---|---|---|---|
| 39% | 40% | 38% | **WELCOMING** |
| 37% | 38% | 35% | Peaceful |
| 36% | 37% | 35% | Spacious |
| 26% | 27% | 26% | Pleasant |
| 26% | 26% | 26% | Condominium-style |
| 13% | 12% | 16% | Cozy |
| 10% | 9% | 12% | Casual |
| 9% | 9% | 9% | Refined |
| 3% | 3% | 3% | Expansive |

(Provided by Luntz Global Partners for Diamond Resorts)

There were also key differences among our members, not only in age, but in gender, lifestyle, family makeup, activity level, and more. We charged Frank with understanding them all.

First, he shared with us the looming distinction between Diamond members and Diamond owners. Members wanted us to add more resorts, in more locations, while owners vocally wanted better amenities and upgrades at existing resorts. It became clear that to satisfy both key constituents of our clientele base, we couldn't have a single focus—we'd need a multipronged strategy to keep a competitive edge.

## Members want **FLEXIBILITY** . . .
## Owners want to **MAKE THE MOST OF THEIR TIME**

### Which makes you **MOST** interested in taking a Diamond vacation?
### (Top 7 Responses)

| TOTAL | MEMBERS | OWNERS | |
|-------|---------|--------|---|
| 43% | 49% | 26% | Vacations where, when, and how you want them |
| 30% | 32% | 25% | Simplicity, choice, and comfort |
| 27% | 28% | 23% | Guaranteed vacations to premier travel destinations at affordable price |
| 26% | 28% | 21% | The most resorts . . . the fewest hassles |
| 25% | 24% | 30% | Relaxation . . . simplified |
| 25% | 24% | 25% | A lifetime of unforgettable vacation memories |
| 20% | 16% | 33% | Make the most of your valuable vacation time |

(Provided by Luntz Global Partners for Diamond Resorts)

For instance, while the majority of Diamond vacationers saw travel as an opportunity to see places and things they'd never seen before, we learned that our female guests were most interested in the memories they'd make, and our male guests were most interested in the fun they'd have in the moment. To us, that translated into ensuring that each of our resorts had places for relaxation and quality time *and* plenty of activities, amenities, and opportunities for the spontaneous adventures you can only have on vacation. It wasn't about being one or the other; it was about variety.

## Vacationers want to see
## things they've never seen before

What would you like most out of your vacation experience?
(Top 6)

| TOTAL | MALE | FEMALE | 18–49 FEMALE | |
|-------|------|--------|--------------|---|
| 27% | 25% | 28% | 21% | To see things I've never seen before |
| 19% | 16% | 23% | 36% | A lifetime of memories |
| 18% | 22% | 13% | 19% | Fun |
| 16% | 15% | 16% | 12% | New experiences |
| 5% | 6% | 5% | — | To broaden my horizons |
| 5% | 5% | 5% | 10% | To bring home great stories |

### Men are interested in FUN, whereas women
### want A LIFETIME OF MEMORIES

(Provided by Luntz Global Partners for Diamond Resorts)

## OWNERSHIP OF THEIR VACATION

Perhaps what was most enlightening of all was the distinction that Diamond owners made about themselves. Did they think of themselves as guests, vacationers, patrons, clients, timesharers, or customers? No. They identified as just that, *owners*.

This wasn't simply a matter of semantics. There's a fundamental and significant difference. A guest, a vacationer, a customer—those are all temporary transactors. But ownership carries a sense of permanence and accountability. And for us, that flipped the script. No longer were we going to think about providing an experience that people looked forward to for a week or two out of the year; we were determined to deliver a Diamond Resorts ownership experience that made people proud of their affiliation with us the whole year through: at our resorts, at home, anywhere and everywhere. That's what true ownership is all about.

We stopped calling our products timeshares because that's not how our members viewed what they were buying. They were buying a piece of Diamond Resorts itself. From then on, our sales presentations centered on vacation ownership. To us, the switch signified a commitment to the respect, understanding, and gratitude that we felt toward our members. We knew they had no shortage of purchase choices; but they were trusting and choosing to affiliate with Diamond Resorts.

**We were determined to deliver a Diamond Resorts ownership experience that made people proud of their affiliation with us.**

## Making the Changes Happen

Frank's research was enlightening because it showed us how to take three hundred thousand voices and condense them into a road map for improvement that every guest and owner would appreciate. But you may be thinking, "It's one thing to do the research and another to implement it."

To that, I'd say you're absolutely right.

| | | What Diamond Owners Really, REALLY Want |
|---|---|---|
| 1 | | More locations and options than any other company |
| 2 | | No wait at check-in—GUARANTEED |
| 3 | | The **most value** for what you spend |
| 4 | | A place where you can relax and unwind |
| 5 | | A home-away-from-home experience <u>every time</u> |
| 6 | | A dazzling array of different choices and options at the resort and surrounding area |
| 7 | | You <u>deserve </u>the best, we're <u>committed </u>to giving it to you. |
| 8 | | It's your vacation. It's our pleasure. |
| 9 | | Spacious accommodations with a view |
| 10 | | The control and flexibility of ownership |
| 11/12 | | Treats every guest with respect and dignity/Treats every guest like family |

(Provided by Luntz Global Partners for Diamond Resorts)

The changes we undertook were monumental in scope: commissioning new decor, modernizing rooms with new and stainless-steel appliances, ensuring the Wi-Fi service reached each room reliably. To show our customers that when it came to our mission to convert Sunterra properties into Diamond Resorts, we meant what we said and said what we meant—we added special touches to let them know that not only had we listened but also that, yes, we had acted.

That's why when you stay at a Diamond Resorts International property today, the bed linens and towels are embellished with a small diamond design. Do they add to the functionality? No. Do they show our guests we are proud of the changes we've made, enough to literally put our stamp on them? Yes. This was our way of saying, "We hear you. We value your input. You can count on us to deliver the value you deserve."

---

## We added special touches to let them know that not only had we listened but also that, yes, we had acted.

---

Despite all this, something inside screamed that these cosmetic changes were only the beginning. Yes, they're important—they deliver on the propositions our customers had told us mattered so much to them:

- Our guests said they cared about comfort, so we went above and beyond to provide comfort.

- Our guests said they cared about choice, so we updated all our resorts, ensuring that anywhere they wanted to travel, they'd be met by the same standards at their favorite resorts.

- Our guests said they cared about simplicity—which we believed meant that they craved true peace of mind—so we looked for ways to create that from the ground up.

We knew, though, that for us to be able to keep focusing on the customer and delivering experiences of value, we would need to find a way to sustain the high bar we'd set. So we continued to fine-tune our thinking about what our guests needed and the way we did business. In so doing, the purpose and heart behind the Meaning of Yes continued to develop and take shape, and we began to zero in on the next principle of hospitality.

### The Final Word

- Including your customers in the corporate decision-making process takes courage to start and perseverance to implement.

- Customers deserve to know that you not only listen to them but also act on their behalf.

- If your customers can't count on leadership from the top, they won't count on service from any tier of the organization.

# Commit to Continuous Improvement

# From a Culture of No to the Meaning of Yes

I was intent on rebuilding Diamond Resorts into something of incredible quality, something unprecedented in my industry at that time. I had carefully listened to my guests, embraced the changes that were needed, and begun to develop new ways of living and practicing hospitality. I believed our focus would always need to be on the guest, and I soon realized that to execute this, we would need to enlist the people who could best carry out the Meaning of Yes across our business: our employees.

This chapter is about how we came to empower our teams and how in turn, they revolutionized the hospitality industry.

## Learning from the Best

When you think of excellent customer service, who do you think of? A few businesses that come top of mind for me are: Amazon, Google, Zappos, and Nordstrom.

I've known Linda Nordstrom, granddaughter of the illustrious company's founder, for many years. In fact, I consider her a neighbor. And though our industries may seem extraordinarily different, listening to her stories about retail changed the way I think and work today.

The first thing Linda will tell you about the family business is that the true secret to its greatness wasn't in the concept, the merchandise, or the marketing. It's in the people. And I agree with her.

Consider the following about Nordstrom:

- Salespeople rarely point. If you're lost or looking for a specific item, they will walk you there. And if you can't find what you're looking for at Nordstrom, salespeople will do their best to help you brainstorm where you might be able to find it—even if that means helping their competition.

- If you make a purchase, salespeople walk your bag around the counter and hand it to you personally, rather than just pushing it toward you across the sales desk. That's their small way of showing respect and appreciation for choosing to shop with them in a time when you have more retail choices than ever before—both brick and mortar *and* online.

- If you call a Nordstrom location or service rep, departments are trained to answer the phone before the third ring. No going to voicemail. No being put on hold. No wondering if you'll talk to a real person.

These may sound like small, inconsequential acts, but together they create a shopping experience that's personalized, humanized, and individualized. This is the recipe for a shopping experience that's simplified and hassle-free.

So how did the Nordstrom brand—which was founded in 1901 and now operates 122 full stores in the United States and Canada—develop such a strikingly consistent reputation for customer service, not just throughout the years, but across states, territories, and stores?

> Small, seemingly inconsequential acts come together to create an experience for customers that's personalized, humanized, and individualized.

It wouldn't be illogical to think that Nordstrom must have a robust and thorough salesperson training program, one in which new hires learn the strict rules of the road and practice delivering top-notch service for hours on end. But you'd be wrong. Nordstrom's success stems from the tone it sets with its employee handbook, which every new hire receives and is tasked with reading in full.

Luckily for employees, this "handbook" is no more than a simple card—one that takes all of ten seconds to read.[1]

The "handbook" no bigger than an index card says, *"Use good judgment in all situations."* Nordstrom employees know their mission is to help every customer who walks through the doors, whether the customer is simply browsing or on a committed shopping spree. Guided by this North Star, Nordstrom salespeople are afforded the respect, license, and empowerment to do what's right in the moment. There's no checking protocol. There's no asking a manager first. Employees know their job is to simply deliver what a guest is asking for, efficiently and effectively.

Linda's example taught me that burdening my people with suffocating rules, guidelines, and regulations would only snuff out the spirit of hospitality that had called them to this line of work in the first place. If I truly wanted to make Diamond Resorts International the best it could possibly be—if I truly wanted our name to become synonymous with excellent guest service—then I knew we had to find our own North Star, one that would encourage and empower our people to do the right thing for our guests, each and every time.

## Committing to Our Employees

I had my work cut out for me. In talking with my customers, I had opened myself to their honest feedback—both positive and negative. And there was one word I heard repeated that I grew to resent more than any other.

"*No* sir, we don't have that."

"*No* ma'am, unfortunately that's not something we do here."

"*No*, I'm afraid that's not our policy."

It became clear to me that the one word our people had gotten accustomed to saying most of all was *no*. Staff had been conditioned under Sunterra's leadership that policy was more important than people. This had to change.

A culture of no is a culture of losing. No one spends hard-earned dollars to be rejected or given a list of excuses when they ask for perfectly reasonable accommodations or alterations. No two guests are the same. Why should we treat them as if they are?

What's more, I find it very difficult to believe that anyone actually enjoys saying no. Our team members were drawn to the hospitality industry in the first place not because they loved resorts, but because they loved people. They had the spirit of service in them already, but it had been buried under Sunterra's pressure to cut costs and cut corners, sell a product instead of deliver a service, and win a buck instead of engender loyalty.

We owed our team an apology—and a commitment from the top that the culture of no wasn't going to be tolerated any longer.

### LEADING BY EXAMPLE

Whereas we've all heard horror tales of new management acquiring a company and cleaning house, at Diamond, we made a point of not letting anyone go for a full year after the acquisition deal was finalized. It wasn't out of generosity; rather, this decision was born out of a realization that this year was my chance to prove myself to my team members.

Just as Diamond Resorts had to regain the trust of guests and owners that had eroded under Sunterra, we had to demonstrate our commitment to our team members again. This year was an opportunity not just to outline the changes we'd be making but to listen to our people, incorporate their feedback, and lead by example. I needed this year to learn from them as much as they needed this year to understand the changes we'd be making. It was a win-win situation and one of the best business decisions I ever made.

As I traveled from resort to resort, I split my time between getting to know my guests and helping my team members. If I walked onto a property and we were short-staffed at the front desk, I hopped behind it. I answered phone calls and set wake-up calls, I made bookings and recommended restaurants. And when a guest asked for something as simple as a late checkout or extra towels to be brought to their room, I said yes.

The ripple effect was tremendous. I carried a guest's bag to the luggage cart—and the next thing I knew, the staff did the same for the next family that arrived, and the next.

When I walked around the pool, I straightened towels on lounge chairs and picked up books that had fallen off side tables so they wouldn't get wet on the ground. After that, team members who worked inside the restaurants began helping their colleagues ensure the pool deck was tidy; and deckhands on a rainy day helped our restaurant staff roll silverware.

Between recruiting the right candidates and retaining top performers, role modeling serves as a reminder to all staff of the service and performance you expect. And when you say yes to delivering great customer service, suddenly confining job boundaries and labels become less meaningful. You do what you can, not what you're told, and that immediately began to make all the difference.

Between recruiting the right candidates and retaining top performers, role modeling serves as a reminder to all staff of the service and performance you expect

If you don't believe that such small changes could truly make a bot-tom-line impact, let me share another example of this with you.

Richard Anderson became Delta Airlines' CEO in 2007, right after the company emerged from bankruptcy. Morale was down and so were profits. Not only was he attempting to reverse course from the lowest point in the company's history, but for the sake of competitiveness, he orchestrated a merger with Northwest Airlines the following year. For the consolidation to be successful, Anderson had to consider business plans and also create a cohesive culture of cooperation and service.

I'll let the company's performance speak for itself: Anderson turned the once-hobbled airline into a global powerhouse. In 2015, Delta earned $4.5 billion in net income and became the industry leader in on-time per-formance. (For anyone who's been delayed at an airport for hours or even missed a connection, you know how much this matters.) In January 2016, for instance, when much of the East Coast was buried by an enormous snowstorm, Delta's percentage of flights not canceled, a measure known as mainline completion factor, stood at 98.7 percent. More than 85 percent of its flights still landed on time.

That's huge.

But how was it possible? Aviation industry wonks have their theories, but I have mine. Anderson was the number one proponent of his people. He never accepted special treatment for himself—he was known for flying coach—but he always touted their accomplishments. He preached delivering a premium product for all travelers, regardless of where they were going, how much they paid, or how often they flew. His mantra? "You value the people, you value the customer, and you give your employees the tools and direction that they need."[2] If that's not a pure expression of hospitality values at the highest level, then I don't know what is.

Anderson led by example and gave his people what they needed to do their jobs better than anyone else. In my estimation, that's the reason Delta continues to lead the rankings in financial performance and reputation when it comes to domestic airline carriers today.

The Meaning of Yes was born from a simple commitment to give our team members and our guests the experiences they deserved. We believed that we had the right people on our staff because they had all chosen to enter the hospitality industry. Working with people, delivering great service, making those around them happy—that's not a career; that's a calling. (More on this later.) We believed that we could do more to enhance the guest experience simply by giving our people the respect and empowerment to make the right choices in the right moment.

## The Final Word

- Small, seemingly inconsequential acts come together to create an experience for customers that's personalized, humanized, and individualized.

- Afford employees the respect, license, and empowerment to do what's right in the moment. The moment a team member must ask permission to do what's right is the exact moment you know your corporate structure is being crippled by undue bureaucracy.

- A culture of "no" is a culture of losing. Like improv acting, the better answer is always, "Yes and?"

- No two customers are the same, so why treat them as if they are? Embrace individuality.

- A business zeal toward cutting costs and corners too often leads to a culture of underdelivering service and undoing customer loyalty.

# Prioritize Reputation over Brand

# Empower the Periphery

The secret behind the Meaning of Yes is that it's *not* a revolutionary idea—it certainly never was meant to be. Just like Nordstrom tells its people to use good judgment and Delta tells its people to value their customers, the Meaning of Yes is designed to be easily understood, universally applicable, and immediately actionable.

You can't effect consequential change without clearly articulating your vision for the future. The idea may be simple, but the results were and continue to be staggering. Within a few months of rolling out the Meaning of Yes, guest satisfaction metrics shot up across the board and across our resorts network-wide. Employees told me they were happier at work than ever before, which re-energized their sense of professional purpose. You could see it on their faces, you could hear it in their laughter in the canteen hall, you could appreciate it when guests wrote notes thanking our staff for doing what staff loved to do—saying yes.

This happened because we prioritized our focus on reputation rather than on brand. In our desire to grow as a company, we didn't lose sight of our customers or the heart behind our kind of hospitality. We spent more time cultivating an experience and building our reputation than we did just talking about our work.

## Instilling the Meaning of Yes

The successful rollout of the Meaning of Yes wouldn't have been possible without my chief experience officer at the time, Patrick Duffy. Patrick's sole focus was not simply explaining but instilling the Meaning of Yes within every department, every property, and every team member.

Of all the ways to do it, he chose the analogy of a cupcake.

As Patrick traveled the globe giving presentations to our sales and marketing teams, he brought cupcakes with him to each stop. He placed them up where everyone could see them—but no one could reach them as he began his talk.

"I think it's safe to say, ladies and gentlemen, that most of you here—whether you've been with the company for four days or fourteen years—have been schooled in corporate rules and regulations, terms, conditions, policies, and procedures."

At this point, heads began to nod, and a few involuntary, audible groans usually escaped. Would this be another corporate compliance drill?

"And I bet you know how to rule and regulate every solution, resolution, question, query, no matter what it is," he continued while walking over to the baked goods.

"That's the 'cake' in the cupcake. Yes, it's necessary. Yes, there's a right way to go about it. Yes, it matters.

"But it's the icing on top that makes a cupcake special and memorable. It's what you include with the basics, the 'more' you add to the must-haves that makes you come back for seconds. That's what this company is all about." At this point, he handed out the cupcakes to the team members in the audience as he started to explain the tenets behind the Meaning of Yes.

# The Meaning of YES®

**Patrick C. Duffy**
Chief Experience Officer

(Source: Diamond Resorts)

Opening slide of Patrick's TMOY presentation deck.

No wonder his presentations always had such rave reviews. He was able to effect consequential change at Diamond Resorts because he so clearly (and creatively) articulated our vision for the future. The ripple effects of his messaging were tremendous.

**You can't effect consequential change without clearly articulating your vision for the future.**

## The Effects of Reputation over Brand

The best part of Patrick's job, at least according to him, was listening to stories from our guests who experienced the Meaning of Yes firsthand. There are troves of accounts that detail how our staff goes above and beyond to make our customers' stays more enjoyable, comfortable, and memorable. From handling the hassles of making early reservations so a family could start their vacation right away, to bringing a British couple a teakettle in Lake Tahoe to make the Sierra Nevadas feel a bit more like home, to sending complimentary flowers and a bottle of champagne to couples who shared that they were celebrating a honeymoon or anniversary. But of all the stories, from all the resorts, a few that Patrick has collected over the years simply stand out. Take a look at these, and I think you'll see why.

• • •

We have just returned home to the UK following a two-week holiday in Arizona. For our first week, we stayed at Sedona Summit, where we thoroughly enjoyed the beautiful surroundings of the Sedona resort. It was our second week at Rancho Mañana, Cave Creek, that moves us to send this email. This resort provided a real sense of retreat, with a stunning pool area and some of the best Diamond Resorts accommodations we have encountered. However, it was the outstanding personal service provided by the resort management that we would most like to acknowledge.

On our arrival, we discovered that our cell phones were not working in the area and we were unable to make international calls from the resort. Without a second thought, the resort manager let us use her own personal cell phone each afternoon of our stay, so that we could contact our daughter back in England and let her know how we were getting on. This provided us with the reassurance we needed that things were fine back home. Her pleasant, professional, and caring manner at all times has left an extremely positive impression of the resort. We were left in no doubt that we were important to her. Staff of this quality, who are prepared to go beyond what is required of them, continue to make Diamond Resorts special.

• • •

I'm writing to tell you about something I observed at the Ka'anapali Beach Club in Maui that should be brought to your attention immediately.

I was relaxing and enjoying perhaps my second or third mai tai from the pool bar when, out of the corner of my eye, I started watching an outdoor Ping-Pong match orchestrated by your activities team members. Several children were playing, and their laughter was a lovely background noise as I was sunbathing and leafing through a few magazines. But suddenly, the laughter paused. Curious as to why the game had disbanded, I looked out from under my sunglasses to see what was happening.

What I saw made my day.

One of your activities team members had crouched down next to a young boy in a wheelchair, who must have been watching the Ping-Pong tournament for some time. I don't know what she whispered to him, but suddenly, his face lit up with joy. He grabbed the paddle out of her hand, and she wheeled him to the table. Next thing I knew, the laughter picked up again—and his was the most discernible of all as your staffer spotted him to victory.

There's no shortage of reasons I love my time with Diamond Resorts—the sun, the waves, and, yes, the mai tais. But most of all, I love coming back to a place year after year that takes genuine care of people and makes everyone feel welcome.

Hope you don't mind that I marked this email with high importance. I thought you deserved a reminder of just how amazing your staff can be.

•••

As a transplant New Englander, I've always dreamed of trading wintertime pine trees for the surf, sand, and palm trees of the beach. Trading eggnog for piña coladas. Stockings for sunburns. Tacky sweaters for swimsuits.

Which is why I couldn't have been more ecstatic this past December to pack up the kids and celebrate Christmas at Diamond Resorts' property down in Baja Sur, Mexico. From the Spanish architecture to the coral reefs to the whale watching, making our Christmas a holiday destination was a dream come true for me.

But even though my children were older, I noticed a change in mood as we got closer to Christmas Eve. And when I finally asked them as we were standing in the majestic Cabo Azul entrance way, next to the beautiful hibiscus floating in the reflection pool, why they weren't smiling in paradise, my daughter told me it just didn't feel like Christmas without a tree. I was taken aback. Yes, this was my perfect Christmas, but it hurt to hear she was missing home.

Our family departed for dinner in town, and I tried not to think of it for the rest of the night. And by the looks of it, my daughter was doing the same.

So imagine our surprise when we walked into the room and found a palm tree strung with white lights. On the counter was a card that read, "From all of us at Cabo Azul, we wish you a Merry Christmas. Please enjoy your very own Mexican Christmas tree."

Next year, we're already talking about how we can bring a small palm to New Hampshire so we can always celebrate the holidays with our very own Mexican Christmas tree.

Thank you for making our family's Christmas one to remember.

## From Micromanaging to Mastery

At the beginning, the old guard at Sunterra was admittedly skeptical that we'd be able to build a business based on trust and collaboration instead of the stress, hierarchy, and micromanaging that had previously ruled Sunterra. Where were the revenue projections? The cost-cutting sell-offs? The meticulous data regressions and overwrought strategy sessions? Still, their reservations were the least of my concerns. I knew the Meaning of Yes at Diamond would never reach its full potential if our team members didn't love what they did each and every day.

Here's a concerning fact that should give us all pause: The rate of heart attacks goes up significantly across the world on Monday mornings.[1] Rather than being excited about the activity that makes up the bulk of our day—our work—too many people see it as something they have to do just to make ends meet rather than something that can be a means of providing economically and producing genuine appeal and interest personally. They're anxious. They're fed up. And they're paying for it with their health.

> Internal culture was once shrugged off as a "soft" business consideration. Today, it's a definitive and strategic competitive advantage.

No company can succeed in the long term if its people are unhappy. Unhappiness breeds resentment. Resentment leads to cutting corners. Cutting corners is an onset symptom of marketplace complacency. And complacency is the death knell of all good businesses, regardless of size, industry, or budget. Internal culture was once shrugged off as a "soft" business consideration. Today, it's a definitive and strategic competitive advantage.

From the age of eight to today, I never viewed work as a means to an end—for me, it has been a source of value, meaning, and, yes, sustenance. I wanted the same for our team members. No one should go to work already

At my house, every year we celebrate Passover, the holiday that memorializes the experience of Jews as slaves in Egypt and celebrates their deliverance from bondage. We read from a liturgical text called the Haggadah, eat ritual foods, and reflect on this history as if we experienced it personally in our own lives.

My family uses the traditional American Haggadah, sponsored by Maxwell House Coffee since 1932. (I will note that President Obama apparently used the same kind at the White House's annual Seder from 2009 to 2016.) My favorite passage comes early in the evening. It reminds us that *we* were in fact strangers in Egypt, and therefore must welcome strangers to our own Seder. We recite, "Let all those who are hungry, enter and eat . . . all who are in distress come and celebrate."[2] For those wondering why we'd send out an invitation for others to join when we're already gathered at the table together, I'd offer the explanation that the invitation is for ourselves. We may all be physically present, but a reminder to be mentally, spiritually, and emotionally present is always warranted in these hectic times. Our bodies may be still, but our minds are wandering. This invitation asks us to be truly present in all forms and interpretations.

Hospitality's emphasis on the importance of taking care of and empathizing with others goes a long way back. These beliefs are ancient. They speak to how we treat others in times of crisis; Passover's themes of freedom are as relevant today with the world's refugee crisis as they were millennia ago. But they also underscore how we may treat others in calmer times, in our own lives, with smaller acts of goodwill.

Remembering what it was like to be a stranger is not only important at Passover. We are told time and time again in the Jewish scripture to show kindness toward strangers. The Torah warns against harming a stranger; I believe the official count nets out between thirty-five and forty-six distinct times, depending on how you choose to translate. In Exodus, we're told, "You shall not wrong a stranger or oppress him, for you were strangers in the land of Egypt."[3] (Elsewhere in Exodus, this is written as "stranger in a strange land"[4]—which, by the way, is the inspiration for the title of the popular science fiction novel by Robert Heinlein.)

Judaism is far from unique in its deep regard for the stranger. In his description of the last judgment, Jesus says, "I was a stranger, and you invited Me in."[5] Later, in the Epistle to the Hebrews, we are advised: "Do not neglect to show hospitality to strangers, for by this some have entertained angels without knowing it."[6] Again, the relevance to today's times is undeniable. Imagine if all strangers, all foreigners, immigrants, and refugees, were treated as if they were divine messengers.

There's an ancient Hindu scripture that says, "The guest is equivalent to God."[7] Hospitality to guests and strangers—called *Manushya Yajna*—is one of the "five great sacrifices" to be carried out daily, according to Vedic practice.

And so, too, the Qur'an instructs Muslims: "And do good unto your parents, and near of kin, and unto orphans, and the needy, and the neighbor from among your own people, and the neighbor who is a stranger, and the friend by your side, and the wayfarer."[8]

Hospitality is a theme reverently discussed not by one religion or within a certain set of beliefs; but rather, hospitality is part of the human tradition itself. Its implications are as all-encompassing and granular as we let them be. But every act of hospitality—from welcoming strangers, to caring for travelers, to simply making guests feel comfortable—is work that is deeply personal, empathetic, and innately rewarding.

Hospitality is a calling.

counting down the minutes until a shift is over and they can punch the clock. Work, if you're open to it, can be a place of community and meaning as well.

Let me illustrate my point with this short parable of three bricklayers:

When asked, "What are you doing?" the first bricklayer replied: "I'm laying bricks." The second bricklayer, pointing at his fine crafts-manship, answered: "I'm building a church." The third bricklayer responded, with pride in his voice: "I'm raising God's work."

Some people have a job: something they *need* to do. Others have a career: something they're *good* at. But the lucky ones? We have callings: something we feel compelled to do because it's in our nature, because it's part of what makes us whole. Callings are something we would continue doing, regardless of employment. In my industry, I believe that those who are drawn to hospitality are among the lucky ones who have a true calling to take care of others. The work of taking care of others is a theme that knows no chronological or cultural boundaries.

True hospitality is essential not just to one faith, belief system, or culture—it's essential to the entire human tradition.

Cooks, front desk agents, activity counselors, and more had come to Sunterra partly because they wanted to work in an interpersonal environment, one where relationships matter and small gestures don't go unnoticed but instead are celebrated. They had the intrinsic motivation that would ultimately propel Diamond to new heights of success but that had been nearly extinguished by the unrelenting emphasis Sunterra as a company had placed on extrinsic motivators: sales, annual returns, profit margins, growth percentages, new acquisitions. All the right people who had all the right inclinations were told all the wrong things: Focus not on what you came here to do because taking care of people is part of who you are but, rather, sell; skimp during your entire shift in order to make the system more lucrative.

No one enters hospitality with dreams of over-promising and under-delivering; people in guest services come to this field because providing for others is rewarding, fulfilling, and meaningful.

The mismatch between Sunterra and its leadership led to a culture of micromanaging. Team members were no longer confident that what they knew was right by the customer would be approved by the company. And so, rather than reach out to make the enterprise better, they remained tied to specific job duties and tasks outlined strictly by their roles. Managers, to take care of properties and resorts—where any hotelier knows no two days are the same—adopted checklist and "helicopter boss" norms that made team members feel even more unappreciated and undervalued. And at the executive level, work streams were siloed and separated because cultural trust had all but eroded. It wasn't a virtuous cycle but a vicious one, in which team members at every level of the company felt constrained to predetermined roles with little room for self-expression, growth, or capacity to make a difference.

For us to succeed, we had to get back to a place of trust and teamwork. And that had to start at the top.

## COLLABORATION, COMMUNICATION, NO STAGNATION

For a company to be truly great, I believe the whole must be greater than the sum of its parts. Diamond achieved cultural cohesion by emphasizing three key ideas:

Collaboration, Communication, No Stagnation.

One of the first changes I made to the company's leadership structure was the creation of what we called the E-Team. The E-Team was a board of both senior leaders and team members from nearly every operational area the company has. It put people together who had never met before, let alone worked together and collaborated to solve complex, company-wide problems. From our chief experience officer, to treasurer, to controller, to

IT director, to marketing director, to food and beverage director, to chief of staff, to communications director, to director of creative services: The E-Team was a board of thirty-two diverse divisional leaders who would come to work with one another, not against one another.

It's amazing what simply bringing people together can do.

With time, heads of departments started sharing their projects and initiatives with other department heads. They were more open and up front with issues they encountered and opened themselves up to asking for outside help. Where before, they had only battled for resources and attention, the culture of increasing collaboration led to new ideas for better serving guests—so much so that we had to institute a rule that each E-Team member could only bring their three best ideas per meeting for group discussion, mostly due to time limitations.

But the most important outcome of the E-Team's creation wasn't the circulation of best practices, information sharing, and strengthened focus on key, company-wide priorities. It was the organic rebuilding of trust.

## It's amazing what simply bringing people together can do.

Executive staff seeing what was possible by embracing Collaboration, Communication, No Stagnation gave more bandwidth to individuals under them. Managers, now feeling less restricted by artificial quotas, felt less pressure and more opportunity to enact the changes that were right for their properties, their departments, their people. And team members, now beginning to recognize that the organizational change underway was more than lip service, embraced their new roles not just as staff but as Diamond Resorts Ambassadors. This meant that everyone at the company, regardless of level, tenure, or position, was a fully empowered representative of our brand, company, and, most important, reputation.

Just as the pivot in terminology from *timeshares* to *vacation ownership* was critical in changing the way we looked at our guests, the shift from *employees* to *ambassadors* and *team members* changed the way we looked at ourselves. Both brought something new to the table—pride.

From the first steps our guests take on our properties, it's the people greeting them who set the tone for their immediate guest experience and for their perceptions of the Diamond brand as a whole. If the entrance isn't perfect—if the reception isn't efficient and friendly, if there's no valet or luggage carts available, if an initial request goes unanswered—it can ruin what should be an enchanting and special experience. It's up to our team members to deliver the Diamond Resorts promise—hospitality at its finest—every day, for every guest.

It's our team members—not the buildings, not headquarters—who are the living, breathing embodiment of what Diamond Resorts is and what sets us apart. Whether front-of-the-house, back-of-the-house, guest-facing or not, we choose to call our team members ambassadors as a reflection and in recognition of their importance, and, I hope, a show of the deep respect and gratitude we feel for the passion they bring every day.

The switch from *employees* to *ambassadors* was no mere matter of nomenclature. It was a reminder and a setting of expectations that in hospitality, working another "job" isn't living up to the best of who our company can be. Ambassadors don't have roles; they have responsibilities. And at Diamond, ours is to ensure that every guest has a great vacation, whether it's their first time with us or their fiftieth, by embracing the Meaning of Yes. Team members have the license and the autonomy to do what is right for the guest in every unique situation, because we know that's also the right thing to do for our guest, our people, and our business. By choosing to enter the world of hospitality, our ambassadors show us that they've always had the calling.

## The Final Word

- The Meaning of Yes is designed to be easily understood, universally applicable, and immediately actionable.

- A "yes" culture helps team members feel more confident at work and re-energized in their sense of professional purpose.

- Team member empowerment means emphasizing three core attributes in the workplace: collaboration, communication, no stagnation. It's your team members—not your buildings, programs, or brand—that are the living, breathing embodiment of your company. They establish your reputation and set you apart.

- Internal culture used to be a "soft" business consideration. But it can offer your company a definitive, strategic, and competitive advantage.

# Ensure Total Alignment

# Embracing a Collaborative Meritocracy

W e set out to deliver the Meaning of Yes so our guests would receive the experiences they deserved. But we were most pleasantly surprised to discover that delivering the Meaning of Yes made us better as a company, as departments, and as professionals, too.

That's because, in short order, the Meaning of Yes eroded traditional hierarchies both at our resorts and within corporate operations. You could no longer say, "But that's not my role," or, "That's someone else's responsibility." When you take on ownership of the Meaning of Yes, you do what it takes to do right by the customer. Full stop.

In the years that followed, I saw that growth and innovation didn't necessarily come from the people with executive titles but from the people who develop new ideas, execute them, and improve them over time. The Meaning of Yes proved that the most common operational structures and traditional hierarchies can hinder performance more than they can help it, just like traditional promotion and recognition systems.

The alternative? Collaborative meritocracies.

## The Merits of a Collaborative Meritocracy

When businesses set out to coordinate human behavior, they tend to do it via chain of command. During the growth of large corporations, many organizations adopted the military philosophy: positional authority based on hierarchy.

But just because hierarchy is the organizational status quo, does that mean it's the optimal organization? Not in our line of work. Day-to-day success was far too situational for us. We couldn't box people into predictable daily tasks and assignments, because in truth, no two days at any two of our properties are ever the same.

For the economy at large, as jobs grow more complex and more dependent on human skills and judgment, not automation or repetition, I expect an explosion in the number of organizations that aren't formal hierarchies. No one has a monopoly on good ideas; and that's why entrepreneurs (like Mark Zuckerberg of Facebook, Steve Jobs of Apple, John Mackey of Whole Foods) tend to appear out of the woodwork.

Everyone talks about meritocracy, but few companies actually build one.

It seems like common sense that you'd want to crowdsource more ideas from more people within your organization. Implementing more effective and efficient approaches is a function first and foremost of generating new ideas and possibilities in the first place.

Think of it: Are you likely to produce a time-saving, cost-reducing, experience-enhancing new product on your first try? Unlikely. When it comes to inventing new ways of doing things, quality ideas often emerge only after you've come up with your fair share of bad ideas.

By opening the door to contributions from people at all levels in your organization, you're more likely to spot emerging talent early.

## PROMOTING FROM WITHIN

There's no better example than my friend Troy Magdos. When I was at Polo Towers, Troy was going to school for hospitality and hotel management, and working in the kitchen washing dishes and running food to gain experience.

But it didn't take long to see that Troy had more to teach than he did to learn. He got in early and left late. He developed a new, more efficient method of handling the kitchen's inventory. When an appliance broke in the middle of a service period, he didn't panic; he found a way to fix or work around the problem until cooler heads could prevail.

He didn't have the title, but he made the contributions. His work and his work ethic spoke for itself. He gained influence not just in the food and beverage department, but throughout Polo Towers, because he developed a track record of making smart suggestions. In some organizations, there are people you listen to because you have to; at Polo Towers, you listened to Troy because you knew you had something to gain by hearing him out. He focused on earning a reputation, not climbing to a new title. He's a great example of how good ideas can emerge from any level of an organization.

Troy ultimately rose to become a senior vice president of engineering and life safety at Diamond Resorts. Because we believe that talent comes in all forms, from all places, we were able to spot, retain, and elevate Troy to the positions where he could use his abilities to make a larger impact.

> The best ideas emerge from all levels of your organization, if you encourage them.

The most successful business leaders I know like nothing more than to promote from within. Not only do they think it's the right thing to do; frankly, they think it's the *smart* thing to do. By pushing power to the periphery and giving our employees and team members the license to solve problems, take on challenges, and contribute to areas outside their traditional roles and responsibilities, we find that leaders earn followers organically. Other team members gravitate toward emerging leaders for advice. New hires look to leaders for direction. Managers bring leaders onto their teams because they know they're reliable.

## ACHIEVEMENT FIRST, ADVANCEMENT SECOND

Collaborative meritocracies, in which traditional roles are fluid in the name of a higher common goal, make it easier to spot emerging talent and support the right people. This flatter organizational model focuses your team members on achievement first, advancement second.

> Collaborative meritocracies, in which traditional roles are fluid in the name of a higher common goal, make it easier to spot emerging talent and support the right people.

Consider how many times you've heard traditional managers operating in traditional hierarchies complain about millennials. The criticism is as predictable as it is repetitive. "These kids all want to get promoted. They all think they deserve to be CEOs after six months on the job."

What's really happening is that these team members are expressing a desire to be heard, to be recognized, to make an impact. But in a traditional hierarchy, the only path to influencing is promotion.

This is not so in a collaborative meritocracy. Here, people build and earn influence without the artificial prerequisite of moving up the company ladder in rank, title, or tenure. What I've seen to be true time and time again is that our younger team members simply want an outlet for their ambition. We deliver that by encouraging the best ideas—wherever they come from, whoever they come from—to steer our operations, and, in time, for the best brains to build a followership. It's about contributing, influencing, leading: These are the incredibly fulfilling parts of a job that a title could never offer.


## LEVERAGING WHAT YOU HAVE

No one understood this concept better or more intuitively than Mike Flaskey who today, not coincidentally, serves as Diamond Resorts International's chief executive officer. I first met Mike at what was intended to be an introductory dinner. We were looking for a new chief marketing officer at the time, and several recruiters suggested that Mike's track record, experience, and ambitiousness might make for an interesting fit. So, we met for a meal.

Right away, I was struck by how aligned our business philosophies seemed to be. First, you recruit *the* best. Second, you train them to *your* best. Third, you motivate them so they perform at *their* best.

I didn't need to preach this concept to Mike. He knew it. Actually, he *lived* it. He had been a star collegiate baseball player and could have made it to the majors if he had pursued the sport. (And don't let him tell you otherwise—he can be too modest.) But though his path took him to rise through the ranks at Starwood Vacation Ownership and Fairfield Resorts (now Wyndham Vacation Ownership), he never forgot what he learned on the field as a three-time captain: All-star teams aren't made by individuals; they're made by leadership that lifts everyone to perform better together than they could on their own.

Mike was more concerned about how we could leverage the people, the culture, and the intangible assets Diamond Resorts already had than with the changes he could make on his own. He was already thinking of innovative ways we could enrich the sales and ownership experiences. In essence, he came up with a pilot program, Events of a Lifetime, at our first meeting.

Today, Diamond Events of a Lifetime are catered, unique events held exclusively for our members. Think meet-and-greets with Baseball Hall of Famer Reggie Jackson, intimate private concerts with country singer Cole Swindell, golf tournaments alongside your favorite PGA pros. If you've attended one, you know there's no limit to what we can do in these above-and-beyond experiences. And now you know that they were designed by Mike, even before he officially joined the team.

It was this imagination, this creativity, and this commitment to infuse hospitality into all components of the guest experience that told me all I needed to know. I offered Mike the job that night. And a few short days later, he accepted.

> The right people, in the right positions, have the power to transform an organization for the better. Talent is the best investment any business can make.

The rest is Diamond Resorts International history. By placing his trust in Diamond's collaborative meritocracy, Mike's leadership was no small part of our unprecedented success. He put the right people in the right places to make a difference, with his guiding North Star firmly focused on how his team could better serve the guest and infuse timeshare with true hospitality. Like Mike, I believe that putting the right people in the right positions has the power to transform an entire organization for the better. Talent is truly the best investment any business can make.

But don't take my word for it. Consider one of the most far-reaching changes Mike made in his first weeks in his role: the implementation of the Diamond Clarity program.

## DIAMOND CLARITY

Everyone who buys with Diamond Resorts today is part of what the company calls the Diamond Clarity program, a process that ensures each and every individual is treated with the respect they deserve, receives a comprehensive understanding of the agreement they're entering into, and always knows their rights during sales and closing. It's a crowning commitment to remake timeshare in Diamond Resorts' own image, one that rests on integrity, directness, and sincere appreciation.

Here's the wording from Diamond Resorts:

Diamond Clarity™ is a new national program that formalizes a series of new and existing customer-enhancements that define how the company engages with current and future members during the sales and closing process, setting a new standard in our industry. It is built on two core principles: transparency and accountability, and it begins with a simple PROMISE.

Diamond PROMISE memorializes a series of operational procedures and enhancements in a single document that will be provided to all customers at the beginning of every sales presentation. Knowing their rights and knowing what Diamond Resorts representatives will and will not do throughout the sales process gives existing and potential members better control of the decision-making process.

With this clear, concise, and consistent information, consumers can easily determine whether the Diamond Resorts hospitality experience is the right decision for them and their family.

### Diamond Clarity™ Promise—DiamondRESPECT

We know that first impressions are everything. That's why we aim to consistently exceed expectations from day one.

For many of our members, attending a presentation at one of our high-quality resorts was their first introduction to Diamond Resorts and the incomparable hospitality we offer.

After listening to your feedback, we set about refining our sales and marketing programs with a single, defining principle in mind: respect.

*(continued)*

Respect for your time . . . respect for your preferences and opinions
. . . respect for what matters to you.

While other companies make promises, we deliver.

This is DiamondRESPECT:

Transparency

- We will provide clear, concise, and consistent information at our
  presentations so that you can easily decide whether committing to
  vacation ownership is the right decision for you and your family.

- You will receive a summary of maintenance fees charged to members
  of the Collection associations for each loyalty level over the past
  five years.

- We seek to articulate the benefits of membership so you
  understand:

  - The various benefits associated with each loyalty level.

  - How to use your points to book accommodations as well as
    access additional selected hotels and cruises.

  - How to take advantage of/book Events of a Lifetime®, the
    Diamond Resorts Concert Series, and Diamond Resorts Dinners,
    where available in your country/region.

  - How to use your points for other travel arrangements, such as
    airfare, or (for our Platinum members only) how to apply them to
    maintenance fees.

  - How your maintenance fees are being used to ensure that we
    offer our members and owners resorts of the highest quality with
    the latest amenities.

Integrity

- Diamond Resorts International's focus on hospitality at some of the leading resorts in the world and our strong reputation, integrity, and credibility are the cornerstones of our business and set us apart from other companies in the industry.

Directness

- At each presentation, you will be provided with the following materials:
  - Paper copies (or, if requested, copies viewable in real time on a tablet or similar device) of:
    - Purchase documents
    - Governing documents for your review prior to signing
    - Any country state-specific regulatory documents governing the purchase
- You will be given sufficient time to review the purchase agreement and supporting addendum before signing.
- You will meet with a Quality Assurance officer before signing any purchase documents. The Quality Assurance team is independent of the sales organization, and their compensation is not tied to the sale of a vacation membership.
- The Quality Assurance officer will review all documents with you and ask a series of questions to ensure the following has been clearly explained:
  - Any applicable policy regarding transfer of the timeshare interest to a third-party and the fees and costs associated with such assignments.

*(continued)*

- How to use points for travel and other ancillary benefits.

- How to use points for the payment of maintenance fees, if applicable, including disclosure of the exchange rate of points to maintenance fee dollars in such transactions.

- Procedures and deadlines for saving or borrowing points from year to year, and the timing for use based on loyalty level.

- Duration of the membership.

- That maintenance fees are billed annually, must be current to make reservations, and are subject to annual increases in accordance with the project documents and applicable law.

- All consumers have the right to ask a Quality Assurance officer any questions they may have about their rights and obligations prior to signing any purchase documents.

The Diamond Clarity program, incidentally, stems from one of the other principles of hospitality that I think is also crucial: Caring for your reputation (what others think about you) matters more than branding and marketing (what you say about yourself).

The shift in focus has made a clear difference. Today, roughly *60 percent* of new Diamond vacation-ownership sales come from *existing* customers. These are individuals who so enjoy their experience with us that they want more. And this figure doesn't even include the sales from word-of-mouth referrals—current guests, owners, and members telling friends, families, and neighbors about what they get with Diamond and suggesting that it would be the right fit for them, too.

At the risk of getting too far ahead of myself, the future for Diamond Resorts International is bright with Mr. Flaskey at the helm. As I said earlier, recruit *the* best. Train to *your* best. Motivate so team members perform at *their* best.

After seeing how the Meaning of Yes changed Diamond Resorts' culture by making it flatter and more collaborative, it's hard for me to understand why companies still cling to traditional workflows and organization charts. Your people who work alongside one another are best suited to determine who the real leaders are. Real leaders are plain enough to spot: They're the people who get stuff done, who step up when others step back, and who make everyone around them better too.

> **Recruit *the* best. Train to *your* best. Motivate so team members perform at *their* best.**

For those of you who've taken introductory economics or management courses, I trust you've learned about supply and demand curves, equilibrium, and how competition leads to "natural selection" in the marketplace. But I'd remind you of the secret your professor likely keyed you into on the last day of class: Namely, that all these economic models you've been studying so diligently are "lies that can only help you see the truth."[1] Or, in simpler framings still, "The real world is messy."

Traditional management hierarchies assume that motivation doesn't matter, that people are always rational, that experience leads to positive impact. Collaborative meritocracies challenge these presumptions and replace them with a belief in trusting people. Does this model look messier on paper than a typical org chart? Absolutely. But that's okay because the real word is a messy place. You need leaders, not preset rules, to navigate it.

### The Final Word

- Truly adopting the Meaning of Yes erodes the bureaucracy of traditional hierarchies. It puts faith in people first, systems second.

- What emerges are "collaborative meritocracies" in which traditional roles are fluid in the name of a higher common goal, making it easier for leaders to spot emerging talent and support the right people. Collaborative meritocracies focus team members on achievement first, advancement second.

- Talent is the best investment any company, in any industry, can make. It starts with recruiting the best people, training them to your best, and motivating them so they perform at their best.

- The best ideas emerge from all levels of your organization, if you encourage them.

# My Business Card on Every Front Desk

By now, you've heard me talk about the difference between jobs, careers, and callings; the importance of pushing power to the periphery; the embrace of collaborative meritocracies. If you're asking yourself what holds all these unconventional structural practices together for a multinational, disparate enterprise, I have one word for you: accountability.

The Meaning of Yes rests on the principle of accountability. Diamond Resorts gives its people the decision-making power to do what's right for the guest, in the moment, because internally we've rebuilt the trust that holds us together. This trust is our most precious strategic asset.

Too often, I've noticed, accountability is discussed in negative terms. It's associated with "answering" for one's actions or rectifying those of others. But by framing it positively—as "this is your domain, what you're in control of creating"—accountability can actually be an invigorating concept. I believe that to achieve success, we need to view accountability as an opportunity rather than a consequence.

Over his lifetime, the acclaimed American educator, businessman, and author Dr. Stephen Covey inspired millions with a simple message: For true success and purpose, we must be principle-centered in all areas of life. A teacher at heart, he told people, "Accountability breeds response-ability."[1]

> View accountability not as a consequence but as an opportunity.

From the Oval Office to the boardroom, from city halls to schools, from small businesses to family rooms, people tend to rise to the expectations set for them—however high or low that might be. By setting high bars and giving our team members the tools, resources, and assistance they need to reach them, I'm always surprised by the talent, innovation, and results that team members produce.

But this is something that's easy to say, harder to do.

## Radical Accountability

I was determined not to be one of those CEOs who was content to preach from the mount. And so, against the advice and admonishments of "foolishness" from my executive team, friends, and business counselors, I decided to do something that would show not only our guests but also team members how truly committed I was to radical accountability.

I announced that I would put my business card—with my personal cell number and direct email address—on the front desk of every Diamond Resorts International property.

"Stephen, that's lunacy—you're going to be inundated with calls and emails."

"You can't do it all."

"Imagine the precedent it will set."

"We don't have the infrastructure—you're setting us up to fail."

"No one's done this before."

"What's wrong with how we tackle correspondence now?"

"Stephen, can you just listen to reason?"

This is just a trickle of the warnings that poured in. And while there were a million possible reasons *not* to put my business card out in the open, there was one reason that, to me, trumped all the other cautions, admonitions, and words-to-the-wise. Simply stated: If I was going to ask my team members to embrace radical accountability, shouldn't I be willing to do the same?

In my mind, the gesture was an equal show of respect for our guests and for our team members. If actions truly speak louder than words, I hoped this simple act communicated three messages: (1) you matter, (2) I have your back, (3) your interests aren't only in mind but also at heart.

My top business advisors predicted deluge levels of correspondence and unreasonable guest requests (free stays, luxury amenities, special treatment) to come pouring in. But what happened was precisely the opposite.

In announcing this action to our team members, we saw more employees in more places do more to *proactively* optimize the guest experience. If I was going to be accepting calls and answering guest emails at all hours of the night, they had every license and reason to ensure that these messages were positive in tone and content. And when I did get complaints or special requests, we were able to judge them on their merit and handle those cases directly. There was no bureaucracy. There were no middlemen. There was no protocol. It was just saying yes to doing right.

Across the board and across the world, we saw guest satisfaction increase. We heard more stories of more team members going out of their way to deliver small acts of kindness to guests and, what's more, to each other.

In short, because we set high expectations for ourselves—from the CEO to entry-level valets—our people delivered.

Imagine, for a moment, if business leaders in other industries embraced radical accountability. If CEOs of banks took customer calls, would employees of Goldman Sachs, Bank of America, Wells Fargo, and the like prioritize profit over people? If CEOs of pharmaceutical companies heard from the families of loved ones who depended on the medicines they make, would we still hear of soaring price shifts in times of economic downturns? If for-profit university presidents heard from alumni who worked two jobs but still couldn't make a dent in their student loans, would the price of tuition creep upward year after year?

I don't pretend to have the answers. But I *do* know that embracing radical accountability and opening up direct communication from guests and team members about their concerns, experiences, and priorities made me a better leader. What's more, it made Diamond Resorts International a better organization as a whole. And it can do the same for you and your business.

Radical accountability frames responsibility in positive terms: What more can you achieve when you take true ownership? By that same token, just as accountability is often framed in the negative, we tend to look for defensive reasons to justify sticking to the status quo before opening ourselves up to the possibilities of "what if?" My advice to you is: Be wary of the status quo when it builds roadblocks between you and your end customers. The closer you can connect to their expectations, the more you set up your organization not just to meet them, but to exceed them.

> Radical accountability frames responsibility in positive terms: What more can you achieve when you take true ownership?

## Simple Ideas, Big Impact

The Meaning of Yes is a simple idea with big implications. It's not a saying but a demeanor, a philosophy, an outlook. I can say with full confidence that Diamond Resorts International's success today is owed to those four little words, all they stand for, and the changes they led to, both dramatic and detailed.

That's because our people understood that embracing the Meaning of Yes meant embracing the truth: Our team members were our company's true leaders. When one of our guests has an interaction with the concierge, in their mind, they're having an interaction with Diamond Resorts. When one of our guests appreciates the immaculate housekeeping, again, they're having an interaction with Diamond Resorts. And when one of our guests calls the front desk with a problem, they're trusting that Diamond Resorts will present them with a solution.

---

**I can say with full confidence that Diamond Resorts International's success today is owed to those four little words—the Meaning of Yes—all they stand for, and the changes they led to, both dramatic and detailed.**

---

The Meaning of Yes banded a network of separate resorts into a company that stood for something bigger, something more purposeful. It reignited our team members' passion for hospitality that had almost been snuffed out by Sunterra and reconfirmed to our guests and owners that we were committed to delivering what a vacation *should* be and *could* be.

The Meaning of Yes united our team members in a common cause, working toward a common goal. It showed us that we could generate *value* by being true to our collective *values*.

Little did we know just how much we'd rely on these four simple words in the months to come.

### The Final Word

- Be wary of the status quo when it seems to build roadblocks between you and your customers. The closer you are to them, the closer they'll stay to you.

- Branding is what you say about yourself. Reputation is what others say about you. Always focus on reputation over brand.

- Radical accountability—focusing not just on consequences but on opportunities and ownership—makes us better leaders and better organizations.

# Do Well by Doing Good

# Taking the Long View

I'll never forget it. It was four o'clock p.m. on a Tuesday afternoon in December. Two business associates and I walked out of the tiled foyer of Fortress Investment's New York City offices at 1345 Avenue of the Americas to the black but bustling New York City streets. Already, it was dark outside. And for someone who called the Las Vegas desert climate home, it was cold—so, so cold. A mix of snow and rain showered lightly from the sky, catching the glint of the skyscraper lights before the drops pooled on the concrete sidewalks. I remember thinking to myself that it was almost pretty.

I fumbled for my gloves in my coat pocket as someone next to me lit a cigarette.

"This," James Weissenborn, who had transitioned from Sunterra's interim CEO to one of my most reliable business advisors, said, "is not good."

"We're going to be fine," I told him.

"Stephen, there's no credit. There's no financing. There's no . . . *nothing*."

"That's why we bought a business that has exactly what it needs—years of due diligence went into this deal."

"We both know that might not be enough. Hell, all of Wall Street is worried about keeping the lights on," he said.

"Good thing we don't have any of our resort properties in Lower Manhattan then."

"That's not funny, Stephen. Jokes, now? Look, I hate saying this, but I give us three months."

"We've got the talent. We've got the strategy. We've got what it takes."

"Maybe six months, top."

"You're taking the wrong end of this bet," I told him. "You'll see."

"I hope you're right."

This was December 2008, only weeks after Lehman Brothers—with $639 billion in assets and $619 billion in debt—filed for bankruptcy. That was not just the largest corporate collapse in US history, but in history, *period*.[1] While others were reading headlines and gawking at how the fourth-largest US investment bank of its time could collapse, my team was frantically studying the subcurrent. As houses were being foreclosed on and hardworking families were losing everything, we knew the Lehman Brothers' fall would make already untrustworthy economic ground even more treacherous. A watershed moment was unfolding before us, one that could accelerate the seemingly unstoppable washing away of market capitalization from global equity markets beyond repair.

In plain English, we knew this was economic DEFCON 1—*not* the situation you want to find yourself in after shelling out $700 million to purchase a once-bankrupt company in the midst of reinventing itself.

How far would the economy spiral? No one dared guess. (In the end, best estimates suggested a loss of somewhere around $10 trillion in capital, worse than our worst-case scenarios ever predicted.) But this chapter isn't an account of the roiling of the financial markets from 2008 to 2012. Tomes have already been written on the subject.

SEP • 62

Stephen Cloobeck and his father, Sheldon, in the fall of 1962.

Stephen in his college years at Brandeis University. He would graduate by the seat of his pants, learning only years later that he suffered from undiagnosed dyslexia his entire academic career. (Part of the proceeds from the sales of this book will go to dyslexia research and awareness efforts.)

Stephen on the construction site of Polo Towers, located in the heart of the world-famous Las Vegas Strip.

Inspired by his children, Stephen would go on to ensure Diamond Resorts would take special care of its youngest customers.

Top: Stephen enjoying a quiet moment with his sons, Jaden and Jake.

Bottom: Stephen with his daughter, Tatiana.

More than 200 Strip frontage property owners unanimously approved the Las Vegas Boulevard Beautification Project, a $13 million special improvement district project that had no fiscal impact on individual taxpayers.

Members of the LifeScapes International team designing a model of the Las Vegas Boulevard. Their work would ultimately come to be designated as a Nevada Scenic Byway, consisting of 4 ½ miles of streetscaping now known as the most recognizable median in the world. *(Photo credit: LifeScapes International.)*

After acquiring the financially troubled Sunterra in 2007, Stephen would transform the company and its portfolio of resorts to launch Diamond Resorts International. On July 19, 2013, DRI would IPO on the New York Stock Exchange Market.

Stephen with President Obama, discussing the private-public partnership created by the Travel Promotion Act of 2009. Today, Brand USA is credited with generating billions of dollars in economic activity. *(Photo credit: Kelly Fajack.)*

This is an account of how we survived the worst economic dearth in modern history and grew to redefine not just itself but an entire industry.

## Doubling Down

It's been said that we can't change the cards we're dealt, only how we play our hand. And from experience, let me tell you that this holds equally true in Las Vegas and in life.

Everyone has their own story and memory of the 2008 financial crisis (or as we all have come to know it, the Great Recession). The shared reality of the day was dislocation. The recession knocked families out of homes, pushed hardworking professionals out of jobs, and shook the faith in the cornerstones of the American economy for each and every one of us. For a young company with huge responsibilities to our team members, our vendors, our owners, and our guests, there was no swifter test to our values, beliefs, and principle-centric business practices.

A 2010 report in the *Journal of Travel Research* using multiple data sets on tourism from 2004 to 2009 looked at how the financial crisis affected travel. Consider the following facts regarding the United States from this report:

- Tourism within and to the United States fell steadily in the year and a half following the September 11, 2001, attacks. "Over the six quarters from peak to the fourth quarter trough, real travel demand fell by 9.5%. In contrast, the nation's real GDP rose by 1% during this period," the report stated. From this low point, demand grew at a rate of 3.7 percent per year until reaching a new peak in the third quarter of 2007. At the same time, real GDP lagged, growing just 2.7 percent a year.

- The current economic downturn began in December 2007; by early 2009, the GDP of the United States fell by nearly 4 percent, the severest decline since World War II.

- By the first quarter of 2009, real travel demand had fallen 6 percent over six quarters. The report read, "This drop so far has been considerably milder than what had occurred after the 9/11 attacks. But the decline has been at twice the rate as real GDP has fallen."

- Tourism employment accounted for nearly six million jobs in the first quarter of 2008. From then through the first quarter of 2009, more than 250,000 jobs in the sector were lost.[2]

To further complicate matters, the impact to the hospitality industry was by no means "even." Places like Mexico saw an uptick in travel between 2008 and 2012 as people flocked to less expensive destinations. But trips to Europe and similarly priced excursions fell drastically, as families looked to conserve funds on travel.

During this time, the Meaning of Yes and complementary reforms we made were still relatively new. Everyone—our team members, our guests, our owners—was still adjusting. As a young company facing a crisis, we had a choice to make: Should we double down on our beliefs when we didn't know how long it would take the economy to recover—and indeed, economists and commentators were questioning not just how long, but if the modern economy would *ever* recover—or should we change course, saving cultural amends for a calmer time? Having weathered all the disconcerting news of 2008, our team realized we had not only a business choice to make but also a responsibility to send a clear signal to our members, guests, and owners that the global financial crisis would not affect their experiences at our properties.

We realized they needed this time at our resorts perhaps more than ever before. At that point, we could see that they had been taking less and less time, and regrettably, that's been the case ever since the recession. On average, Americans are now leaving a full seven vacation days unused and on the table.[3] That's a week every year that's supposed to be dedicated to rest, relaxation, and rejuvenation—and we're choosing to avoid it. Even in routine years, vacations have been linked to significant health benefits for the overworked, hyperstressed, and overbooked among us.

> **Their resolve, their dedication, is the real reason Diamond Resorts International didn't simply make it through the financial crisis when dozens of other timeshare companies folded, closed, or entered bankruptcy—they're the reason we emerged stronger and more committed to one another than ever before.**

Those years weren't without pain for our company. As we did our best to serve our guests, customers, and owners with unflinching dedication and commitment, we also needed to make sacrifices in-house. Nothing was more painful than letting people go—and so, wherever possible, we did our best to avoid that outcome as we worked to stay afloat. I asked everyone to stay the course with me, promising I'd do everything I could to get us through to the other side. The company renegotiated compensation plans, and the majority of our team members willingly accepted less if that meant keeping more of our people employed. I'd never been more humbled. Their resolve, their dedication is the real reason Diamond Resorts International didn't simply make it through the financial crisis when dozens of other timeshare companies folded, closed, or entered bankruptcy—they're the reason we emerged stronger and more committed to one another than ever before.

In all this, I also learned that we do well for ourselves when we make sure we do good for others. This is something that's stayed with me ever since, and I've seen time and time again how putting people first and doing the right thing leads to the kind of success that really matters. The fact that Diamond Resorts flourishes as a business is, I believe, a direct result of that.

## "Only Look Forward"

The global financial crisis was a turbulent time for everyone, and as the leader of a company with staff around the world, I can say in all sincerity that I didn't know the meaning of true pressure until those years. I had never come face-to-face with a threat so large, so indeterminate, so outside my power to control. I looked for stories of inspiration, fortitude, and, yes, succeeding against the odds to help sustain our leadership through difficult times. Perhaps no example inspired me more than that of my friend Jim Murren, CEO of MGM.

Jim is known to refer to himself as a fish out of water in the Las Vegas limelight. In 1998, MGM's then controlling shareholder, the famed Kirk Kerkorian, recruited Jim from the East Coast. Kerkorian wanted a level-headed voice for financial accountability, transparency, and responsibility in an industry that was infamously known to play it fast and loose, even with millions in bank loans. But whereas I spent my formative years in the kitchens of my father's California developments, Jim called Connecticut's "Gold Coast" (Fairfield County) home.

The son of a seminarian turned lawyer, Jim graduated from Trinity College in Hartford where he majored in art history and city planning. (To this day, my ever-humble friend calls himself an unsuccessful architect.) From there, he had a ten-plus-year tenure as a stock analyst with C.J. Lawrence and Deutsche Bank before being enlisted to the services of MGM Grand.

People around town know Jim for his low-key demeanor. (He's famous for toting an old-school canvas backpack instead of a briefcase.) People in the industry know him for his ferocious negotiating skills, especially with "bought deals." But I know him for designing the $250 million Nevada Cancer Institute, which he and his wife, Heather, helped establish together.

For the first few years, Jim seemingly could do no wrong. He kept bank loans streaming in, based on a simple but proven-to-be-profitable value proposition possible only in Vegas: borrow the millions you need to build a lavish hotel with a no-expense-spared casino on the ground floor, bedeck it with all the bells and whistles of some over-the-top theme ("gingerbread," as some in the gaming industry call it), and, after opening, proceed to recoup a return on investment of typically 20 percent or more. That meant within just a few short years, developers could pay down debt and do the whole thing over again.

That is, until this entire model was smashed to smithereens in 2008.

To this day, Jim keeps a framed copy of the original concept sketch for CityCenter—a $7 billion project, with $5 billion of it borrowed—that envisioned six condo towers, a casino, and a shopping mall on the mostly vacant land next to MGM's Bellagio casino. The idea was to bring a community of style, swagger, and sophistication to downtown Vegas, the likes of which the Strip had never seen before. In total, the real estate development projection was estimated to cost 40 percent, give or take, *more* than comparable projects in Vegas. The bottom of the framed original concept sketch is dated February 2004.

This meant, as you can foretell, that the recession began as construction was in full swing. Where credit was once a foregone conclusion, now it seemed irretrievably out of reach. For all his efforts, Jim was able to raise only $1.8 billion from the banks. And so, after many late-night phone calls, difficult conversations, and contentious meetings, he sold a half interest in the project to Dubai World for $2.7 billion in 2007.

We'll skip the gory details, but suffice it to say that with one lawsuit, a period of suspended payments, and Dubai World's investment swelling to $4.3 billion, the project that was meant to be Jim's crowning achievement almost broke him and nearly bankrupted the company. (At one particularly tense and trying period, CityCenter was within hours of shutting down if a temporary financial solution wasn't reached in time—fencing had been secured, the Las Vegas Police Department had been briefed, and MGM Mirage's own security force had been prepared. What's more, MGM might have followed the project into bankruptcy if a short-term solution for its $13 billion debt load hadn't been crafted. With only hours to spare, Jim was able to broker a restructuring deal.)

It took everything my friend had learned in business over a quarter century's worth of experience, sage advice from numerous directions, and the sweat-inducing labor of his team for Jim to keep the company from veering off the edge of a financial cliff. But in December 2009, with over sixty thousand people having applied for ten thousand jobs, CityCenter opened its doors to the public. This seemed to be a feat accomplished through one man's sheer force of willpower. In his own words: "It was an incredibly challenging time. It seemed the problems were too big for one company to withstand."[9]

What kept Jim going in all this? He points to a few choice words from none other than the man who brought him to MGM in the first place, Kirk Kerkorian.

During the recession, Kerkorian tried to be a voice of steady reassurance. Jim recalls that Kerkorian called him nearly every single day during the lows of the CityCenter project—usually at night, when Jim was out of the office and could speak more freely. Jim told me the conversations were never long and never went into great detail—Kerkorian meant them as more of a morale boost than anything else—but they were sorely needed. For Jim, one piece of advice stood out: "Only look forward."

It would have been easy in this time for Jim to look back—to assign blame, wish different decisions had been made, even wallow in regret. But Kerkorian's advice was to keep going, even when you could barely see ahead more than one day.

Jim's herculean efforts to salvage CityCenter—to this day, the largest privately funded construction project in the

For those of you who aren't familiar with Kirk Kerkorian, his is a story worth knowing. He embodies the entrepreneurial spirit and resiliency of Las Vegas better than anyone. The son of Armenian immigrants, he had no formal education past the eighth grade. What he did have was a diversity of formative early life experiences—as a pilot, as a boxer, as a voracious gambler—that served as his personal, unconventional education. He leaned on these experiences to defy expectations and succeed on his terms. After serving in World War II, Kerkorian rose from poverty to invest in airlines, car companies, and film studios throughout his career. But from his first entrepreneurial gamble to his last, Kerkorian always bet on Las Vegas. The Strip as we know it today wouldn't be the same without Kerkorian's influence on the hotels and gaming companies. He was a self-made man in every sense and one who gave back magnanimously.

history of the United States—hinged on advice to keep your eyes and head up, even when everyone is betting against you. Lots of people talk about passion being at the heart of different entrepreneurs' and businesses leaders' success. But Jim's example of saving CityCenter (more commonly branded now with an ARIA focus) convinced me that while passion may be necessary, it is not sufficient. Passion (the heart) plus perseverance (the guts) constitutes the character you really need: grit.

On the night of ARIA's grand opening in December 2009, I stopped by Jim's office in the Bellagio before the celebratory events were scheduled to start. And there, as faithfully as ever, was the original framed CityCenter sketch, dated 2004. I had something to present to my friend to kick off the evening that night: a light joke. A few weeks before, I had visited my jeweler and tasked him with making an "unconventional" sculpture, a ten-pound mold of "brass balls" dated 2009 to close the CityCenter chapter. Without the mettle, determination, and fortitude Jim had shown in the face of unbelievable adversity, CityCenter would have been a sketch—and only a sketch. "Congratulations," I said, presenting my friend with this unusual trophy. "You really do have . . ."

After that, we made our way to the ribbon-cutting festivities.

> In business as in life, your passion (heart) and perseverance (guts) come together to give you the grit you really need to succeed.

## Grit over Guts

There's a saying so time-tested it's lost its original attribution. It goes something like this: "Success is 90 percent failure." Indeed, in Silicon Valley, the epicenter of entrepreneurism today, for every single start-up that gets off the ground, an average of nine fail outright. But the near guarantee of failing isn't what interests me. Rather, it's the reason why some businesses, having experienced nearly fatal encounters, are able to recover and succeed when no one imagined they could.

There are also lots of talented and successful people in the world. But what is it about those few who separate themselves from the pack? Albert Einstein, Walt Disney, Oprah Winfrey, and J. K. Rowling may all have fame, fortune, or household recognition, for example. But before each of these successful superstars made it big in their respective industries and spaces, they first failed, were fired, and were met with countless no's. The tremendous struggle, effort, and persistence it took for each of them to achieve success is something worth learning from.

Drawing on her own story as the daughter of an immigrant scientist who frequently lamented her own "lack of genius," the pioneering University of Pennsylvania researcher Angela Duckworth argues that breakout success isn't determined solely by talent but rather a special blend of passion *and* perseverance that she calls grit.

After reading her research and publications, I first recognized something that I had long intuited but been unable to articulate. Enthusiasm (passion) is common. Endurance (perseverance) is rare. And as my time leading Diamond from 2008 to 2012 taught me, and Jim Murren's example with the CityCenter project showed me, the latter makes all the difference in business.

> Enthusiasm (passion) is common. Endurance (perseverance) is rare. Success in any pursuit demands the combination of the two.

We're all capable of short bursts of energy, incredible displays of talent, and flares of genius. (Remember that time in college when you swore you were going to make it as a guitar player? Or a renowned artist? Or really believed you had the invention destined to become "the next big thing"?) These momentary outbursts are necessary but not sufficient.

- Albert Einstein's name may today be synonymous with genius, but in his early years, people doubted whether he showed even a basic level of intelligence. He didn't speak until he was four or read until he was seven, and teachers branded him "slow." Despite the frustration and constantly being misunderstood his entire life, he pursued his true passion: scientific endeavors. He went on to publish three papers that transformed the face of modern physics as we know it.

- The teenage Walter Disney was fired from one of his first animation jobs because he "lacked imagination and had no good ideas."[10] He went on to drive the first animation company he acquired right into bankruptcy. Then later, when he tried to get MGM to distribute Mickey Mouse, the studio told him that the idea of a giant mouse on the screen would never work. Fifty-nine Academy Award nominations and twenty-two wins later, along with the creation of Disneyland (spurring *the* premier multinational amusement park business), the rest is history. Today, the Walt Disney Company averages a revenue of $30 billion annually.

- Most people know Oprah as one of the most iconic personalities of television, as well as one of the richest, most successful, and most influential women in the world. But before her success came numerous career setbacks. She was fired from her job as a television reporter because she was "unfit for television news,"[11] and later from her post as a co-anchor of the six a.m. weekday news after the show received low ratings. Seven years later, Winfrey moved to Chicago, where her self-titled talk show went on to dominate daytime TV for twenty-five years. Far from being unfit for TV, she came to rule it.

- Before J. K. Rowling had any *Harry Potter* success, the writer scraped together a life as a divorced single mother on welfare. She did this while attending school and writing a novel, sharing later in a commencement speech to Harvard University that she was "jobless, a lone parent, and as poor as it is possible to be in modern Britain without being homeless."[12] Suffering under deepening depression, she came to see herself as a failure and began contemplating suicide. But as others were urging her to "be practical" and get a "real job," Rowling stuck to her writing. Today, the *Harry Potter* series has sold well over four hundred million copies, making her one of the most successful and celebrated authors of all time.

As Professor Duckworth argues—and I agree wholeheartedly—it's not intensity but *consistency over time* that drives success. Enthusiasm (passion) is common. Endurance (perseverance) is rare. But success in any pursuit demands the combination of the two.

"But Stephen," I can hear the protesters say, "aren't some people just . . . gifted?"

Look, there's no denying that talent matters: your raw athleticism, a knack for solving math problems, a "gift" for making the right business decisions at the right time. But talent on its own is just one of the many factors that goes into finding real and lasting success. What matters more—actually, double—is the *effort* you put into whatever you're pursuing.

# Talent X **Effort** = Skill
# Skill X **Effort** = Achievement

Grit: The Power of Passion and Perseverance

The more meaningful your effort—the hours of piano practice, extra homework help, time late at the office—the more you grow your skill level. And the more effort you put into applying your skills—trying out for the band or orchestra you never thought you'd get into, taking harder classes you never thought you'd pass, making the tough business calls you considered yourself unprepared to make—the more opportunity you give those skills to do good for others. *That's achievement.*

Talent only becomes skill with effort, because it takes even more effort for skill to manifest newly earned achievements. Precisely because effort counts *twice*, success is more a function of application rather than raw talent. (I note the irony that Professor Duckworth's work on understanding grit has won her the prestigious MacArthur Fellowship—commonly referred to as the "Genius Grant.")

Success in business and in life is a function not of innate *talent*, but of a willingness to draw deep from your personal well of *effort*. Just as even my closest business partners predicted an early fall for me, others will bet against you—sometimes publicly, sometimes privately—on whatever road you start down.

> Success isn't determined merely by how good you are but also by how badly you want it.

But that's why when betting on yourself, you should evaluate not how *good* you are at the outset but how *badly* you want to succeed on your particular journey, over the long haul. That's part of taking the long view of things. That's how you begin doing what it takes to succeed. That's where grit comes in.

Most important, though, remember that as you strive to succeed, it will always go well for you when you're motivated by a desire to do the right thing for others. In my experience, there simply isn't a better way to work.

### The Final Word

- In business, passion (the heart) is necessary but not sufficient to succeed. You also need perseverance (the guts) to get what you really want.

- In times of hardship and adversity, double down on your core values and institutional principles. The instinct all too often is to abandon them.

- A growing body of research suggests that "grit" is the top predictor of professional success. Namely, it's not just how good you are but how badly you want to go after your goals.

# PART THREE

# Once an Entrepreneur, Always an Intrapreneur

W hen I talk to young people today—whether recognized by chance on the street, on college campuses, or in MBA presentations—I try to always ask them what they aspire to be, what trajectory they're on, and where they think they'll land. I admit that it's a bit of a trick question. When these students or young professionals look at me and say, "CEO," "Business exec," "Founder of my own company," or—most commonly—"An entrepreneur," I let their answers hang in the air for a moment or two and then respond with a single word: "Wrong."

You can imagine the blank stares and the slacked jaws.

I try to explain. "People will ask you what you want to be 'when you grow up,' what you're going to do when you graduate, or where you want to end up in life. But I challenge you. If you really want to be a leader, tell these people that they're thinking about it in the wrong way. It's not about what you want to *be*. It's about what you want to *do*. This is the more meaningful consideration that will ensure you're doing what you truly believe in throughout your career. What distinguishes leaders is that they're never satisfied—they're consumed by what they want to do, achieve, and accomplish *next*."

> It's not about what you want to *be*. It's about what you want to *do*.

At Diamond Resorts, I woke up every morning and asked myself this question: How are we, as an organization, going to be better than we were the day *before* so we can do more for our guests *tomorrow*?

When I look back, I see that asking my team and myself this question made all the difference in our work and in our success. Because we were never content, we never became complacent. Because we never were satisfied, we were always looking for ways to improve "the little things" that perhaps no one else noticed. Because we were 100 percent committed to continuous improvement, we were able to listen to and learn from our guests, members, and owners and stay ahead of the competition.

I'm always amazed by myriad headlines dedicated to or describing what it takes to be a successful entrepreneur. Among some of the recent titles that have come across my desk are: "Five Traits of Being a Successful Entrepreneur," "What All Successful Entrepreneurs Have in Common," "Could You Be the Next 'It' Entrepreneur?"

In my mind, these journalists and reporters are wasting ink (and too often, readers' time) by investigating the wrong question. The more interesting and, in my opinion, more telling query isn't about taking on the initial risk of pursuing your own idea or *starting* your own company—it's the *stamina* required to sustain it. The secret to today's leading companies and organizations of every industry, sector, and size isn't one-time entrepreneurship; it's continuous, strenuous, relentless intrapreneurship.

Intrapreneurs promote innovation, get people to rethink the way things work, and look to improve things from the inside out.

Rather than focus on *entrepreneurship*, what if we focused on the long, grinding, never-ending work of *intrapreneurship*? Intrapreneurship is the ongoing exercise of making existing operations run more efficiently and effectively, growing new commercially viable ventures that strengthen the organization as a whole, and, perhaps most simply put, taking what you have in business and remaking it into what you want. Intrapreneurs promote innovation, get people to rethink the way things work, and look to improve things from the inside out.

**Intrapreneurship**
>in·tra·pre·neur·ship
>ˌintrəprə'nər/-ship
>Noun
>The act of promoting innovative product development, creatively rethinking and reshaping current systems to work more efficiently and effectively, and seeking continuous improvement in all corners of the business operations.

Far more important than coming up with the next big idea is our willingness and commitment to reinvent ourselves, our products, and our organizations.

## Profile of an Intrapreneur

Intrapreneurship plays out in lots of different ways, but in my opinion, someone who does this really well is casino magnate Steve Wynn. I believe Steve Wynn has not only changed the face of Las Vegas but also the fortunes of the entire state of Nevada. Even more, he's influenced the cityscapes of some of America's—and the world's—greatest destinations. Today, Wynn is the man behind some of Las Vegas's most notable landmarks: the Mirage, Treasure Island, Bellagio, and Wynn Las Vegas. He's known for his attention to detail, extravagance, and commitment to customers, which is precisely why you might be surprised to learn that Steve Wynn got his start in *bingo*.

> Life isn't about what you've already done—it's about what you have the opportunity to create next. If you *won't* or *don't* push yourself to care about the seemingly unimportant or insignificant details, someone else *will*.

In 1963, following the passing of his father, Michael, who owned a number of faltering bingo parlors in the eastern United States, Wynn took over the operation of the family business. When he took the lead, the company was $350,000 in debt.[1] But through his leadership and operational attention to even the finest of details, Wynn parlayed those halls to raise sufficient funds to move to Las Vegas in 1967, becoming part owner, slot manager, and assistant credit manager of the Frontier Hotel. He saw what worked, what didn't, and what could be improved. In 1971, he was able to make a significant investment in the Golden Nugget Casino, transforming the institution into a AAA Four-Diamond resort known for its elegance and service, all at a time when the gambling industry was more infamous than famous, and more shabby than star-studded.

The rest is Las Vegas history. Wynn never saw the city as what it was (a desert town) but as what it could be (the epicenter of luxury tourism).

Modern Vegas and the gaming industry today were fashioned out of his ever-evolving vision.

> Complacency in one thing leads to complacency in all things. We should fight this in every form.

When I was first preparing to open Polo Towers in the early 1990s, Wynn had already cemented his reputation as the Las Vegas developer. Las Vegas was on the verge of becoming synonymous with luxury—but not quite yet. I remember studying Wynn's developments and resorts that were leading this charge because I admired his work. From the fresh-flower arrangements that became nothing less than works of art to the ornate rugs and decor, I remember standing in sheer awe of the glamour, the ritz, the atmosphere that one individual was able to dream up and make reality. It was unlike anything I'd ever seen or experienced before. Until then, I didn't know you could think so big, imagine so much, and actually make it happen.

Wynn was constantly re-creating his properties, which, by everyone else's estimation, were already great. His example taught me that life isn't about what you've already done—it's about what you have the opportunity to create next. Because if you *won't,* if you *don't* push yourself to care about the seemingly unimportant or insignificant details, someone else *will*. I believe complacency in one thing leads to complacency in all things. We should fight this in every form if we want to make a real difference in the things around us.

## Reinventing and Redefining

To stand out on the Strip where there is, to put it mildly, no shortage of visual stimuli, I made the original decision to design the exterior of Polo Towers in a fuchsia hue that complemented the desert mountains in the backdrop. For anyone in development and design, you know color is one of the most agonizing decisions. There are hundreds of shades in a single hue, thousands of hues in a single color family, limitless color-family pairings and options. Settling on a fuchsia that blended into desert sunsets but stood out from the lights of the Strip felt like a minor milestone accomplishment.

That is, until I saw Cirque du Soleil's *Mystère* in 1993.

The show was a microcosm of Las Vegas itself. Full of daredevil acts, acrobatic impossibilities, and infinite grace, each scene was somehow more transfixing and imaginative than the last. But what I recall the most is the colors. A palm-green stage matched with brilliant, deep costumes and backdrops. It was unlike anything I had ever seen before.

Right away, I knew I had to change Polo Towers.

While no one else thought anything was wrong with the resort's then-current facade—still spotless, still brand new—I pressed forward with a $250,000 makeover. Just as the mesmerizing, deep purple ribbons dangled from the ceiling at the Cirque du Soleil performance, captivating the audience's attention and pulling people's gaze upward as the dancers twisted and turned above the stage, I pressed my engineers to re-create that specific shade of magenta. What I envisioned was not streams of cloth but streams of light that would flank the building, pulling passersby's eyes away from the Strip and onto Polo Towers.

At first, they told me no—it couldn't be done. The color was too difficult to reproduce in LED or neon light technology. No one had done it before. When I heard this, I replied, "Great, when you create it, we'll be the first."

Intrapreneurship requires seeking inspiration from everywhere and anywhere and never settling.

To this day, if you visit Las Vegas Boulevard, you'll spot Polo Towers by its deep purple lights, unmatched by any other structure in the city. To guests, these lights set the tone for the grandeur and extravagance of Las Vegas; to me, these lights are a reminder of what's possible when you seek inspiration from everywhere and anywhere and never settle.

If entrepreneurship is about starting something great, betting on intrapreneurship—the constant reinvention and redefinition of what *great* truly means—has made all the difference in my experience. And as I tell young people I meet everywhere, it can do the same for you.

### The Final Word

- Complacency in one thing leads to complacency in all things. Fight it in every form.

- Ask yourself the same question that effective leaders ask themselves: How can I be better today, so I can do more for customers tomorrow?

- Entrepreneurs often get glorified, but it's the intrapreneurs that get results. They look to improve things from the inside out.

# Remaking Timeshare in Our Own Image

I'm sure you've heard a timeshare stereotype or two. The hours-long presentations. The fast-talking sales representative. The high-pressure "move now or forever lose out on a great deal" tactics. One bad apple is all it takes to spoil the whole bunch.

By the time I entered the business, timeshare—at least the worst forms of it—had already taken on a sort of urban-legend persona. People were afraid of the good actors because the horror stories caused by the minority of bad actors were outsized in scope, belief, and atrocity. Imagine that you're going to look at a resort to consider whether it's the right fit for you and your family, and the next thing you know, you're stuck in a windowless room at the back of the house with a commission-driven agent who says he'll take two hours of your time, which ends up closer to five because he seemingly won't take no for an answer.

What's worse, back in the 1970s and 1980s, these aggressive tactics were all but impossible to escape. Many "resorts" were simply beachfront motel conversions, which were poor values for the average consumer, while fraudulent marketing practices further damaged the industry's image. As a reminder and basic but illustrative example, if a developer built a condo that cost $200,000, he could sell it at $20,000 per week for fifty weeks (fifty different families renting it for one week out of the year) and make $1,000,000. Given that sort of margin, it doesn't take much of a logical leap to see how the timeshare industry became bloated and laser focused on one thing and one thing only: sales, sales, and more sales.

## The Need to Raise the Bar

While these practices may have been lucrative for corporate coffers at the outset, it made for a long-term, hard-to-remove stain on the business model, guest service reputation, and even companies and individuals who went out of their way to buck these bad practices. Because of a few actors' malfeasance (it's hard to say anything other than greed), timeshare itself is increasingly regulated by state governments and watched by the Consumer Financial Protection Bureau.

In Hawaii, for example, state law requires the purchaser to have a seven-day right of rescission of any timesharing sales contract. It outlines specific guidelines for developers, acquisition agents, and sales agents of timeshare units, providing that the failure to fully disclose certain actions as sales solicitations constitutes unfair and deceptive business practices. And the law in Hawaii is also quite severe with respect to seller misrepresentations.

In Florida, purchasers may cancel timeshare contracts up to ten days after the date of contract is signed if the seller is notified of the cancellation in writing. And any attempt by the seller to waive the cancellation right is prohibited. While closing documents may be executed during that time, the closing cannot actually take place until the ten-day cancellation period has expired.

These sorts of laws aren't uncommon today; in fact, they're the rule, not the exception. Most states now have regulations to allow consumers a reasonable chance to change their minds before purchasing rights to a property they haven't fully thought out.

Undoubtedly, these regulations have protected many buyers from purchases they would have later regretted. As wonderful as timeshares can be in creating memories, providing a place of relaxation and escape, and expanding one's world view, like any major purchase, they can be a source of financial and emotional stress if one isn't fully prepared to take them on. Timeshare agreements should be regarded as a long-term investment, not a one-time deal, because in truth, that's exactly what they are: investments.

But as regulations and government rules have provided safety guardrails for industry players, they in themselves can't raise the bar for customer service and guest treatment. It takes good business sense and a company-wide, cultural commitment to the customer—not legislation—to do that. As I pointed out in chapter 8, reputation matters more than branding or marketing. The latter is what you say about *yourself*, but the former is what others say about *you*.

## Remaking Things the Diamond Way

Diamond's self-driven, referral-based sales are a far cry from relying on the high-pressure tactics that once dominated the industry. What got us to this point wasn't swimming with the current but a willingness to stand for doing things differently to better serve the people who matter most: everyone who stays with us, for however long or however brief.

From remaking our sales presentations to remaking our resorts, our actions reflected a willingness to stare down the status quo. The question at the core of our mission was: How can we make the entire experience, from sales to vacation spells, more customer-centric? In short, how can we make every feature of the experience, from booking technology through the travel period itself, closer to the Meaning of Yes?

Let's consider a typical Diamond sales presentation today.


## THE WELCOME

First, when you check into the resort, you're welcomed by our ambassadors with a smile and an eagerness to ensure you're comfortable from the moment you set foot on the property. The front desk greets you, an associate helps get you settled, and you're offered the opportunity—take it or leave it—to sit down with one of our ambassadors who can help familiarize you with the resort, the local area, and a litany of attractions, excursions, and experiences offered between the two.

> Ensuring that good intentions translate into good results starts with active listening. It's about the guest or owner, not about the associate.

If you choose to say yes, you're welcomed into a patio or well-appointed room with plush chairs and sofas (we strive to make our welcoming lobbies a far cry from the cramped plane, train, or automobile you likely took as transportation). You're offered a drink—in England, perhaps a cup of afternoon tea, or in Cabos, perhaps a celebratory tequila, or whatever fits the mood—and asked what brings you to this Diamond Resorts location specifically. Adventure? Amusement? Relaxation? Family? Rather than tell you what you *should* do, our ambassadors are here to listen to what you *want* to do, so they can make recommendations and reservations that fit your agenda, not the other way around. I believe ensuring that good intentions translate into good results starts with active listening. It's about the guest or owner, not about the associate.

Only then, with a few restaurants and activities in mind for you to discover first, are you invited to sign up for a sales presentation at your discretion and on your schedule. Take a few days to explore on your own, or come back when you're well-rested tomorrow for a fully guided tour of the resort and all of its amenities. It's your choice. You're in control. Diamond Ambassadors will be here waiting if you'd like to learn more.

What I advise is that you wait a day or two to survey your new settings on your own. Get acquainted with the pools, the beaches, the on-site restaurants, and the area. This time on your own is important for you to take stock in what you enjoy the most.

## THE EXPERIENCE

Should you decide to partake in a sales presentation, we strive to make it an experience unlike any you've encountered before. From the moment you walk in, there's music playing that adds to the joy of your surroundings, not generic elevator music. Think Van Halen in Vegas, traditional mariachi in Mexico, steel drums in the Caribbean. We want our presentations to elevate your vacation experience overall, not serve as a distraction from it.

From there, you're matched with a Diamond Ambassador who knows the resort and the company like the back of his or her hand. We want every question you have to be answered knowledgeably. And if there's something that stumps your ambassador? A question that goes beyond the scope of their experience or tenure? You're met not with guesses, but with an up-front and transparent, "To be honest, I'm not sure, but I'll be glad to get the right answer for you."

We know your time is valuable—this is the vacation that you've worked hard for, after all. So why waste it in an office space? Our ambassadors can take you for a complimentary meal at one of our on-site restaurants or simply on a walking tour of the entire grounds to ensure there isn't a point of interest you've missed or overlooked. The immediate focus is to get to know you better—your wants, your preferences, your priorities. We believe by getting to know you better, we can suggest the excursions and activities that will make your experience better overall.

Map of Diamond Resorts International Properties. (Pins = multiple properties.)

## THE VALUE IN A VACATION

And then, Diamond Ambassadors will ask you to *imagine*: Imagine what it would mean for your family to have ownership in a vacation subscription that doesn't merely allow but genuinely encourages you to travel the world. A vacation-ownership model that doesn't lock you into one property, for one specially reserved time on the calendar in perpetuity, but that grants you the flexibility to choose the days, regions, and experiences that fit your life as you and your family grow, change, and explore new possibilities together. A subscription that doesn't forfeit a vacation experience and expenditure should circumstances not be amenable one year, but that allows you to roll those points over to doubly enjoy your time away next year, at a later date; or reversely, allows you to "borrow" points from future years to make an extra special trip this year.

Diamond Resorts' points system made a huge splash when it was first introduced, precisely because it was a deviation from the timeshare norm. It would have been easier to conform to the deeded-week model—no exceptions, excuses, or adjustability—because that's what the timeshare industry did and what consumers had come to expect (if not particularly enjoy). But when establishing our systems and unifying our resorts, it dawned on our leadership team that the true meaning of simplicity, choice, and comfort could be extended not just to the rooms and amenities but also to the reservation process itself.

That's it. That's the model: The more you enjoy your time with us now, the more you'll want to join us again later. Genuine interactions lead to heartfelt suggestions and storytelling. Diamond members and owners purchase with us not only for our first-rate locations and attractions but also for the way they *feel* while with us. Like they're at home—only better.

Rather than push people into a sale, we strive to demonstrate the value of vacation ownership and subscription. We engage with our guests and create a level of intimacy that breeds honest recommendations that, in turn, lead to tailored, one-of-a-kind experiences. If you like what you see, hear, experience, and—most of all—feel, the right kind of sales (those in which the buyer is prepared to make a long-term commitment) come organically.

## Making Intrapreneurial Changes

Intrapreneurship comes more naturally if you know who you are and what you stand for. For us, we looked for little ways in which we weren't truly living the Meaning of Yes. It became clear that we could do more to improve the sales presentation—that's often the first experience our guests have with Diamond Resorts as a whole. If they don't understand the Meaning of Yes from the very beginning, why would they sign up hoping to receive it later on? It's a missed opportunity for our business and us. Likewise, with so many resorts operating around the world, why did we have to stick to the mold of a deeded week on a dedicated property? The more we questioned the way things were, the more room we found to challenge ourselves to live up to our stated values. The more we consciously looked, the more possibilities we found to imbue our work with the Meaning of Yes.

> ### Intrapreneurship is staring at things that are and seeing not what is but rather what could be.

Intrapreneurship isn't about the next "breakthrough" idea or the next "home run" invention. Those sorts of disruptions are far and few between, by definition. Intrapreneurship is staring at things that are and seeing not what is but rather what could be. It can be harder than entrepreneurship precisely because you're not starting with a blank state, and it can be slow, grinding, steady work. It's a commitment to continuous improvement in all that you do. But, over time, the combined effect of the small changes can lead to a big difference.

> If you know who you are, the values you stand for, and the value you add to your customers' lives, then you can make intrapreneurial changes that are sustainable, smart, and reputation-enhancing that will touch all aspects of your organization.

Our society has conflated entrepreneurs with superheroes. We've become so focused on the supersized innovations that we forget the advantage of smaller, more niche, and specific changes that add up over time. If you know who you are, the values you stand for, and the value you add to your customers' lives, then you can make intrapreneurial changes that are sustainable, smart, and reputation-enhancing that will touch all aspects of your organization.

## Institutionalized Intrapreneurship

Intrapreneurial, systems-specific ideas, besides remaining proprietary, have empowered Diamond Resorts to pay extraordinary attention to detail.

Excellence means getting the details right in all aspects of the business, from product quality to service. At a certain point, it's simply impossible to improve performance *without* small, bite-size, intrapreneurial ideas.

Consider The Ridge on Sedona Golf Resort, a property in the northern Verde Valley region of Arizona overlooking the former homelands of the great Apache chiefs Cochise and Geronimo. Guests come from all over the world to take pleasure in the unspoiled beauty of this desert. While they want an authentic experience, they also expect exceptional service. Because The Ridge pays extraordinary attention to every detail, and thanks to hundreds of small but meaningful ideas from the staff there every day, the resort delivers.

This doesn't happen by accident. It happens through something I like to call institutionalized intrapreneurism.

Every two weeks, The Ridge hosts a staff-wide meeting. Everyone is expected to show up with at least one idea—no matter how modest—that will improve some aspect of the property's operation. Here are just a handful of the ideas they've come up with:

- Provide alcohol-free sparkling cider for nondrinkers on special occasions.
- Offer in-season fruit as a dessert alternative.
- Paint the outdoor water faucets green and red to differentiate between drinking water and yard water.
- Put a step stool in the tour van.
- Relocate the speed-limit sign so it won't be obstructed by the mesquite bush.

Are any of these proposals going to change hospitality as we know it? No. Together, are these ideas (and the dozens more like them) going to tangibly improve the customer experience at this property? Absolutely. To achieve excellence in big things, you need to pay incredible attention to the small details. And Diamond Resorts team members—not managers—are the ones

who most often spot the little things that add up to big success. Institutional-
izing intrapreneurism in your business simultaneously empowers team members and directs their insight, expertise, and experience at improving your
collective value proposition.

When we set out to redefine timeshare and enhance the customer experience, we were simultaneously building a better way to do business. No matter
what industry you're in, consider how our journey and experience can help
you raise the bar in yours.

### The Final Word

- Ensure that good intentions translate to good results; it's about the
  customers, not you.

- Intrapreneurship is about seeing not what is but rather what could be.

- Commit to continuous improvement in all that you do. Over time,
  small changes—which often come at a lower risk—lead to big
  differences in customer satisfaction and commercial outcomes.

- Excellence means getting the details right, from product quality
  to service.

# Seeking Inspiration from All Places

In the latter months of 2011, our company was confidently emerging from the depths of the financial crisis. For the first time in years, we set our sights toward growth. That meant I was traveling the world not just to check on current Diamond properties but also to acquire new ones.

By 2011, many of our smaller competitors were on the verge of collapse. In the boom years, they hadn't saved sufficiently to draw on reserves to see them through the leaner years. In the interim, properties suffered from disrepair, the result of skipping needed regular updating and maintenance work, which led to a downturn in future sales. With current owners upset, properties in neglect, and limited prospects converting to sales, many management arms were looking for any viable way out, short of bankruptcy.

Looking past the slighted upkeep, we saw opportunity to acquire new properties in the right locations faster than we could build them ourselves.

With the Sunterra takeover in our rearview mirror, we knew we could take over mismanaged properties and turn them into thriving enterprises. (In fact, with our commitment to institutionalized intrapreneurism, it's what we excelled at.) Our strategic bet was that our continued rather than stalled focus on better serving members, owners, and guests would be accentuated by our peers' neglect. We could attract more organic sales by doing more for current customers and showing acquired members the benefit of Diamond Resorts International by presenting a contrast to their previous vacation-ownership experience. That, in turn, would spur another stream of referrals and word-of-mouth introductions.

Or so we thought. We knew it all hinged on picking the right target purchases: places our members wanted to go, with proper infrastructure, and a talented employee base. That meant looking not only for business opportunities but also hospitality inspiration that would charm our guests, in all places.

Word spread that Diamond Resorts International was looking to double down on the "international" end of our name by increasing our multicultural, worldwide footprint, and not only did private resorts soon come calling but also foreign governments.

One such call led to an experience I'll never forget.

In this chapter, I'll tell you about one of the most impactful meetings of my life that changed the way I think about hospitality. It's a lengthy story, but one—as you will see—that has directly informed my approach to growing a business and making the most of presented opportunities. I believe the lessons in this story will help inform the way you approach people and situations in your own life.

## The President of Georgia

It was a rare Wednesday when I was stateside with my family between property visits. My calendar told me I was supposed to go to a local business event near our beach home in Laguna Beach, California. It was supposed to be just your run-of-the-mill networking get-together, a mingling session with different executives in the hospitality world trading industry news, opinions on current trends, and thoughts on what the future held. Always big on clean energy, I drove my Tesla up the coastal bluff high above the Pacific, to beautiful Montage Laguna Beach resort, which sits on thirty seaside acres, found a spot in the parking lot, and walked into the lobby.

The usually serene lounge was abuzz with activity, and the panoramic ocean views were obscured by larger-than-normal crowds. Scanning the scene for a familiar face, I spotted my good friend Noah Mamet, who I had known for years from participation in Democratic circles—he would go on to be the US ambassador to Argentina under President Barack Obama—and asked what was going on. A celebration? A wedding? A reunion of sorts?

"The President of Georgia is here," said Mamet. "He wants to meet you."

What?

I was suddenly grateful for some of the extra airline miles I'd accumulated over the past few months. In my mind, I was able to place Georgia, the former Soviet republic, on a mental map straddling Western Asia and Eastern Europe between the Black and Caspian Seas.

To say it was a surreal moment was an understatement. A few minutes—and, to be perfectly frank, a few frantic Google searches—later, Georgian officials ushered Noah and me to an alcove of the Montage lounge that was surrounded by bodyguards and attendees. There was President Mikheil Saakashvili, dressed in a blue suit and red tie, reaching out his hand to me.

Thankfully, the conversation flowed naturally. We talked about the beauty of the Californian coast and how it compared to that of the Black Sea. We talked about Georgia's budding tourism industry and the attractions it leaned on. I learned that the country was home to more than two thousand mineral springs and over twelve thousand historical and cultural monuments, three of which are recognized on the UNESCO World Heritage List.

The way the president spoke of the country's natural beauty was nothing short of poetic; the pride in his voice when he talked about the pro-business reforms spearheaded in his country was exceedingly apparent. He told Noah and me with distinct regard that in 2007, Georgia's real GDP growth rate reached 12 percent, making Georgia one of the fastest-growing economies in Eastern Europe. What's more, he continued, the World Bank had dubbed Georgia "the number one economic reformer in the world" because it had in one year improved from rank 112th to 18th in terms of ease of doing business.[1] It's now ranked 9th out of 190 countries worldwide.[2]

But still, what did it have to do with me?

The president made a motion to his detail after that, signaling that he was ready to leave. Taking that cue, I reached for my keys as well. I'm guessing that out of the corner of his eye, the president must've seen the Tesla insignia on my keys. He put his hand on my shoulder and with palpable excitement in his voice asked if I really had a Tesla.

"I do," I replied. "Would you like to see it?"

The next thing I knew, Noah, the president of a post-Soviet state, a handful of his entourage, and I were standing outside in the parking lot in the afternoon sun. He inspected the vehicle. I held out the keys.

"Go ahead," I said to him. "It's the perfect time of day for a drive."

I had barely outstretched my hand when the president took my keys, opened the driver's door, and got in. He then headed south on the highway with two members of his team in tow.

Noah whispered in my direction: "Do you . . . think he's going to come back?"

A little while later—maybe thirty minutes—the car pulled into the porte cochere of the resort. The president parked, turned off the engine, and smiling, handed me the keys as he stepped out of the vehicle. He remarked that he thought fondly of Diamond Resorts' work on fostering cultural exchanges and that he would like to personally show me his country and its trademark hospitality. I remember telling him that I looked forward to it, and then with that, he left.

That was it. That was the extent of our conversation.

## HOSPITALITY AS A WAY OF LIFE

Months went by and I didn't hear from President Saakashvili, but neither did I think anything of it. I continued my work in scouting out new locations and also making surprise visits to our current resorts. I happened to be at my Las Vegas home between trips one day when I received a phone call from an anonymous number. I answered.

My longtime security guard, Dale Hinton, who is former British military and thus rarely, if ever, surprised, watched me respond incredulously to a rapid-fire series of queries: "Yes, this is he . . . As soon as possible? . . . Of course . . . We'll keep you apprised of our arrival."

I hung up the phone, looked at Dale, and told him we were headed to Tbilisi, the capital of Georgia, to meet with the president. "When?" he asked.

"Right now," I told him.

I think he may have done a double take.

Noah met us in Las Vegas, and we all got on a plane and took off. After sixteen hours in the air, we arrived at one thirty a.m. local time. The airport was covered in the pitch black of night, as was the city in the distance. We expected we'd just go directly to our hotel to rest for the remainder of the evening, but when we descended the jet bridge, we could see the lights of a motorcade line on the tarmac. We were ushered into one of the vehicles.

**It was the warmest welcome I'd perhaps ever received, and I made mental notes to myself that this sort of hospitality is exactly what we at Diamond should be striving for.**

In broken English, our driver explained that he was taking us directly to President Saakashvili's quarters, where the president was waiting for us. We wound through narrow cobblestone streets that looked like they had been plucked from the pages of a storybook fairytale. We whizzed by Byzantine, neoclassical, Art Nouveau, Beaux arts, Middle Eastern, and Soviet architecture, all interspersed throughout the city. Then we arrived.

I recognized the president immediately. He greeted us at the door, though this time casual jeans and a cotton shirt replaced his blue suit and red silk tie. President Saakashvili welcomed us as if we were old childhood friends. He seemed animated, happy to have us there, and showed us around his quarters, seemingly unfazed by the late hour. He surprised us further when he said we were next heading to the minister of state's home for dinner.

Dinner? It was three a.m.

After a short drive, we were there. They'd prepared a feast for us, and it was not only extravagantly displayed but also incredibly delicious. We drank Georgian wine and toasted with *chacha*, a clear and strong pomace brandy that we learned was popular in the region. Even though I was exhausted, I have to say that it was the warmest welcome I'd perhaps ever received, and I made mental notes to myself that this sort of hospitality is exactly what we at Diamond should be striving for.

I was learning from the president, in the moment.

**I could see that the same hospitality he'd showed me wasn't a performance but something that came naturally to him. He may have been a world leader, but hospitality was part of who he was and why crowds gravitated toward him.**

As the plates were being cleared—something closer to four thirty in the morning by that point—President Saakashvili announced that he'd planned a personal tour of "traditional Georgia" for us the next day. I'd heard nothing but amazing things about Old Tbilisi and was already thinking ahead to exploring the Tbilisi Opera and Ballet Theatre, the Sameba Cathedral, and Narikala Fortress. We thanked him immensely for his thoughtfulness.

Just a few hours later, we set out to explore the old city on foot before meeting with the president. The colors, the aromas, the sights: It was as if we'd been dropped into the middle of a movie set, only this was real. I somehow felt at home and comfortable, even in such a foreign place.

When it came time to meet the president, we saw that he hadn't chosen a church, a restaurant, or a historical building as our rendezvous point. Instead, he'd picked an open field. And waiting for us weren't cars but helicopters. Dale, Noah, and I boarded the helicopter, and we lifted off.

The ride proved to be one of the most vivid memories I've ever had to this day, in any country. We flew above the Caucasus Mountains and followed the Kura River toward the Caspian Sea and Georgia's border with Azerbaijan. As Tbilisi faded from view, the president of Georgia explained that some of the villages we were passing over—bordered by white-capped mountains and verdant valleys—became all but isolated in the winter months when the roads that connected them were overtaken by snow. The view, in every direction, was breathtaking.

An hour or so later, the helicopter descended onto a plain covered by wildflowers. The town, a few hundred feet away in the distance, was streaming with villagers who'd come to welcome the president. Some were dressed in traditional Georgian clothing as a sign of respect and celebration. I remember being struck as I watched President Saakashvili meet people in the town, answer their questions, and ask them questions of his own. I could see that the same hospitality he'd showed me wasn't a performance but something that came naturally to him. He may have been a world leader, but hospitality was part of who he was and why crowds gravitated toward him.

When it was time for a midday meal, we walked together toward the Georgian Orthodox church that stood in the middle of town. We were greeted by the priest, who kissed President Saakashvili on the cheek and ushered us into his own home, right next to the church's grounds. There, we found a U-shaped table prepared for us with a spread that made our three a.m. dinner the night before look like a simple midnight snack. The president explained to us that a *supra*—a traditional banquet feast—had been prepared in our honor.

---

**I felt like I was meant to be there. And I realized that this was exactly the feeling hoteliers and hospitality professionals are always striving to engender.**

---

A Georgian feast? For us? With me sitting between the president of the country and the high priest of a beautiful Georgian village? Just yesterday, we had been in Las Vegas. It was all very surreal.

The endless array of dishes and courses was equal parts daunting and delicious, but what truly distinguished the hours-long meal was the toasts. No fewer than twenty toasts marked our lunch, some of which spanned several minutes in length. The first, as it was translated to me, was to Georgia, the next to God, and then to us, the visiting guests. Even though the language barrier was strong, I didn't feel like a foreigner. Surrounded by a Georgian Orthodox priest and men wearing traditional chokhas, I felt like I was meant to be there. And I realized that this was exactly the feeling hoteliers and hospitality professionals are always striving to engender.

I soon learned that the traditional leader of the supra is the *tamada*, or the toastmaster. His job wasn't only to lead the ceremonial speeches but also to dictate the rules of drinking. Traditionally, the tamada is expected to empty his wine glass with each toast (for his jet-lagged guests, more leeway was given). But we learned that it was absolutely imperative that no one drink from a glass less than half full. The wine flowed as if it was bottomless because, essentially, it was. Our hosts had grown, pressed, and aged their own wine, and they were proud to show off what they had been keeping in storage jugs deep in their cellars. With one toast in particular, the wine was drunk out of what I assumed to be real rams' horns, passed around from one person to another.

Then, there was the sheer quantity of food. It started with *tones puri*, Georgian flatbread that bakes in ovens that seem like holes dug in the ground, accompanied by what had to be dozens of spreads and salads. But this was only the beginning—course after course came from the kitchen. There was *khachapuri*, a traditional boat-shaped fried bread covered in cheese, and *shasliki*, dishes of fresh pork and meat. Inevitably, plates began to pile up on top of one another, a sign of a successful supra. Every time we thought, "Surely, this must be the last course," two more would follow. Despite how full I was, it was one of *the* most delightful and heartwarming dining experiences of my life; dinners at the Four Seasons paled in comparison to it.

I knew I needed to call on the courage to make a toast of my own. I clinked my glass and motioned to the tamada that I too had something to say. The table, in fine spirits by this point, applauded me on. And though my words were few, I felt they communicated everything I so exuberantly wanted to say.

"*Nostrovia!*" Loosely translated from Russian, which my grandfather had tried to teach me many years ago, and which, I hoped, shared some semantic resemblances with Georgian, it meant, "To good health!"

It was my small and poorly accented way of saying thank you. It was a thank you for teaching me that hospitality is a way of life practiced all over the world, a spirit that connects us. I understood that hospitality is universal, and even the smallest gestures can leave the biggest impressions. That meal, the toasts, the food, the conversation, the entire experience of being in Georgia created a camaraderie that has stayed with us long after we got up from the table.

Hospitality is universal. The smallest gestures can leave the biggest impressions.

With night falling, we proceeded back to the helicopters and from there, back to Tbilisi. On the way home, President Saakashvili asked if we had enjoyed ourselves. Georgia, he told us, isn't an easy place for Americans or European tourists to travel to, but he hoped he had shown us that it was indeed a worthwhile destination, full of cultural and natural surprises, delights, and authentic experiences.

> Authentic hospitality knows no bounds, limits, or language.

To this day, I think fondly and gratefully of my Georgian adventure. It has deepened my conviction that Diamond must continue developing the relationships, reach, and infrastructure to show our members, guests, and owners not only where a trip out of the ordinary can take you but also the unexpected lessons it can teach you. In my case, I was offered a beautiful reminder that authentic hospitality knows no bounds, limits, or language.

## Creating a Destination

That whirlwind trip to Georgia made me even more determined to find new locations that would extend a sense of awe and unexpected discovery to our members. At the time, our data showed that our guests most wished the Diamond Resorts roster included a slice of tropical paradise that felt like it was a world away but that didn't take days to travel to. We set out looking for properties and timeshare collections that met these requirements. And wherever that finally took us, I knew I wanted us to deliver authentic hospitality like we had experienced a world away in Georgia.

We decided on a more recently acquired property, Pacific Monarch's Cabo Azul in the Baja California Sur, which we felt had the most promise. Located in San José del Cabo, the resort sat on the most covetable beachfront property you could find. The sheer beauty of the natural setting struck me like a thunderclap: whales breaching, waves crashing, crystal white sand glistening.

It was a disservice that the resort itself had fallen into such disrepair before it came into our hands. But I knew it was about looking past what was in front of me—the obstacles, the obstructions—and instead imagining what it could become.

## REDESIGNING A SPACE

When we took over the resort, it immediately became clear to me that it wasn't just the staff's spirit that was suffering but also the physical amenities themselves, from pools to rooms. The quickest way Diamond Resorts could show our new people that we intended to invest in them, not take advantage of them, would be to take care of the fixes that never should have been allowed to fall by the wayside in the first place.

We set forth with a multimillion-dollar renovation.

In the rooms, we replaced dated decor with local, craftsman woodwork; the chairs and coffee tables were intricately designed and handmade. We knew the oceanfront views were the best embellishments we could offer, so we installed floor-to-ceiling windows and outdoor verandas that blended the outdoors with the resort itself. And since the resort resided outside of town, tucked away in the rolling seaside hills, we doubled down on enhancing the natural tranquility, incorporating white billowing curtains, reflecting pools throughout the pathways, straw-thatched lounges, and palm trees and indigenous greenery to provide shade and ambiance.

Cabo Azul and Georgia are worlds apart, but we took the lessons of being true to place, history, and culture and brought them to our work in Mexico. Our job wasn't to overembellish but to elevate the resort's natural, incomparable beauty.

We wanted the front entrance to set the standard of elegance and sophistication for the rest of our guests' stay. We restored the magnificence of the exterior with a fresh coat of white paint and redesigned the porte cochere to be curvilinear, rather than rigidly straight. By accessing the building on a bowed angle, the focal point to the passageway stood prominently and physically drew you in. The doors that swung open were made by the same local craftsmen, only this time they were designed on a far more majestic scale, without sacrificing any of the intricacy of the woodwork. Completing the renovation was an equally architectural and artistic feat.

> **We took the lessons learned in Georgia of being true to place, history, and culture and brought them to our work in Mexico. Our job wasn't to overembellish but to elevate the resort's natural, incomparable beauty.**

### ENHANCING A SENSE OF PLACE

We also took Pacific Monarch's admittedly uninspired list of activities and completely revamped them into a premier array of "suggested excursions" to ensure our partners were truly best in class. We sent scouts to nearby restaurants to understand the quality and niche of each offering; we hired new executive chefs to ensure the on-site restaurants were offering exciting, elevated dishes that made the most of locally sourced seafood and authentic Mexican cooking styles. (And yes, we paid due attention to the kids' menu this time too.)

We looked for ways to integrate local culture into the resort, from activities, to drinks, to music, and more. The spa, which we renamed Paz, in homage to the state's capital city, went from tired to breathtaking, incorporating natural elements like volcanic stone while also carrying on the interior's exquisite artisanal-woodworking theme.

Oceanfront and overlooking the Sea of Cortez, we knew Cabo Azul would be more than a resort—for some, it would be a beckoning destination for the most exciting and memorable moments of their lives. This was a true *destination*. Reunions, celebrations, and of course, weddings—they'd

(Source: Diamond Resorts)

all happen here. We paid special care to the addition of an open-air wedding chapel at the center of the property for just this reason, purposefully built high and at the forefront of the resort to showcase guests' celebrations, not cast them off to an out-of-sight enclosure, and to capture the best views the property could offer.

Our team saw every opportunity as a chance to enhance Cabo Azul's sense of place. For instance, a seemingly overlooked detail, the stone pavings behind the front desk and along the pathways, took on heightened importance when we decided they shouldn't be laid on their side as typically fashioned but stand tall to symbolize the resort's newfound energy, life, and sense of purpose. Every detail, from cornerstone to pathway stone, we imbued with meaning. We believe that if the design matters and speaks to *us*, it will continue to speak to and entice our guests for years to come. No corners were cut, no excuses were given—and Cabo Azul is now a capping property in the Diamond Resorts portfolio.

Months went into the renovations. Sure, we did more to bring Cabo Azul back to glory than perhaps was needed or what other developers would have attempted to accomplish. But to us, Cabo Azul was the first and shining example of our commitment to acquired properties. It was designed to make a statement, both to our guests who would enjoy the space for years to come and to our newest Diamond Resorts team members who were learning what the Meaning of Yes stood for, for the very first time.

## The Final Word

- Authentic hospitality knows no boundaries, limits, or languages. Even the smallest gestures can leave the biggest impressions.

- In hospitality, the goal isn't to overembellish but rather to elevate and enhance what's naturally appealing.

- Hospitality should be in all that we do. It's a way of living life that connects us as people and adds meaning to our work.

# Going Undercover

During this period in Diamond history, I had been traveling nonstop to newly acquired properties and all our original property offerings. But still, my efforts seemed insufficient to achieve the ends I aspired to; our employee base struggled to shift from a work style of indifference and inattention to a culture of service that believed if we held true to our values, then our business would appreciate *in* value. How could I teach what hospitality really meant—something my time in Georgia proved to me was innate to all of us, across geographic divides—to thousands of nearly simultaneously onboarding staff members in different states, countries, and time zones?

If you hold true to your values, your business will appreciate in value.

While I was hyperfocused on bringing hundreds of team members up to speed, my office had been receiving dozens of calls from one of the unlikeliest of places: a reality show.

In 2010, CBS's *Undercover Boss* premiered directly after Super Bowl XLIV for its initial nine-episode season. In the show, executives or individuals in upper management are asked to disguise themselves, taking on jobs in their own organizations that they're not exposed to on a daily, weekly, or even annual basis. Think Mitch Modell of sporting goods retailer Modell's working as a cashier in one of his stores; co-owner of the Chicago Cubs Todd Ricketts selling hot dogs at Wrigley Field; celebrity chef Marcus Samuelsson as a dishwasher in one of his own restaurants. These are all true examples.

At the same time the show was entertaining, it also provided some interesting perspectives and insights. In some episodes, viewers had the opportunity to see if executives truly understood and empathized with their employee bases. In other episodes, viewers had a chance to see top executives assume humbling roles, humiliating roles even in some cases. And in still other episodes, viewers watched an executive's personal journey unfold from a place of lofty isolation—if unintended—to a place of connection and unity with the people in their organizations and companies.

The show was still pretty new and unproven when producers came calling to see if I was interested. My initial reaction? *No way.* I was too focused on *actual* guests and Diamond Resorts' reputation writ large to wade into the pool of public ratings and TV showmanship. And wasn't the whole thing scripted, anyway?

Call after call came in. The producers didn't seem to take "No, thank you" for an answer—and in truth, I respected that dogged perseverance. But it wasn't until my chief financial officer, one of my closest confidants and advisors at the company, approached me personally about the opportunity that I paid any serious attention to it.

His perspective was that it wasn't necessarily about the viewing public; it was about our employees, who would be tuning in. TV provided exactly the personalized medium we were looking for to connect and resonate with thousands of people, all over the globe, authentically and directly. I had the unique opportunity to model precisely the sort of behavior I expected from each and every staff member who put on a Diamond Resorts uniform.

It took cajoling, it took nudging, and to be fully honest with you, it took a few late-night calls to work out my panic and nervousness, but finally, I committed to the idea. Production would take a full week of shooting, with eighteen-hour days.

## Difficult Reality

For anyone who thinks of *Undercover Boss* as a scripted reality show, let me tell you, it absolutely is *not*. Show producers Eli Holzman and Chris Carlson were so secretive about my workloads and planned itineraries that I didn't know which resort I would be visiting, let alone my alias. I was kept in the dark about all the show details up until the first day of shooting . . . which, mind you, did nothing for my nerves.

From the start, some of my misgivings seemed to be materializing. Rather than give me a quality costume, I was given a moppy brunet wig and a pair of glasses to "conceal" my true identity. Didn't these people know that my picture and business card were on every front desk at every resort?

Assuming the character of "Jack Fisher," the production team told me that my first stint would be at Los Abrigados, one of our resorts in Sedona. It was a property I had acquired out of bankruptcy nine months before, so I was eager to see how well the staff was adjusting to the Meaning of Yes. I was to tell colleagues and team members at the resort that we were filming a show about career transitions, and they thought they were supposed to help me assess whether I had what it took to succeed in hospitality.

On day one of shooting, I was given a heavy blue shirt, utility cargo shorts, and, yes, white tube socks. I was starting out as a mechanical engineer on-site. Under the scorching heat of the Arizona sun, I met a resort engineer by the name of Randy, intended by the show to be my first mentor. He listened to me explain that I didn't have any technical experience but agreed to take me on as an understudy anyway. All our plans for the show almost backfired that day when an air-conditioning unit I was attempting to repair unexpectedly burst into flames on the roof of Los Abrigados' fitness center. Without Randy's quick thinking and even quicker action, the first day of *Undercover Boss* shooting would've literally gone up in flames.

But we recovered and went about our day. As the hours dragged on, I learned that Randy wasn't only working at Los Abrigados, but at UPS as well. His wife similarly was a teacher who had picked up a second job at Home Depot. Why? An RV business they had poured their hearts into was lost during a bad transaction. Everything they had saved for retirement was lost with it. As someone who had scraped by in business before, that story more than resonated with me. It cut me to my core.

But here's what they didn't show in that first episode: The first day of work was so grueling, so emotionally draining, that I got into a broil with the show producers. (After eighteen hours of shooting in a scratchy wig, how many more outtakes do you really need?) They didn't know me, and I didn't know them, and all it took was a few heated words to blow up faster than the AC unit. I had reached my limit, not even twenty-four hours in, and I flew home to Las Vegas that night.

To the production crew's credit, one of their team members drove through the night to meet with me in the morning. I had felt disrespected. Even though, to protect the integrity of the episode, they couldn't disclose upcoming details, they promised to be more forthright about the process. It was a good-faith olive branch that I accepted, fully admitting that even one day in my employee's shoes was enough to drive me to a breaking point.

## Trying Again

To make up for lost time, that afternoon we set off to a fulfillment call center in Miami. When people think of vacation ownership, they often think of the front desk, the housekeeping, the resort managers. But in truth, the entire experience starts with reservations. Think of how infuriating it can be to be told no or, "Those dates are blacked out" even before your vacation has begun. The experience *starts* with the ease, choice, and satisfaction of the reservations process, not after it.

After only moments on the phone, it became clear to me that the call center representatives had not been trained with that mentality. Staff did the bare minimum required of them, rather than going above and beyond to meet—never mind exceed—the customer's expectations. A call dropped without the customer knowing the full possibilities of the points program, typos that misled the customer's search, a severe unfamiliarity with the product: We all make mistakes, but we do our best to limit them. At this call center, mistakes were par for the course rather than the exception. And when one particular representative told a consecutive three of my members no, rather than finding a way to say yes, I hit my limit once more.

> The Meaning of Yes is meant for our team members as much as for our customers. Our focus on one shouldn't come at the expense of the other. The two are intertwined.

Right then and there, I ditched my cover and my alias. She wasn't sitting with a trainee—she was sitting with the CEO and founder of the company.

Each of the situations that had gone wrong on the phone were rectified and apologized for by Diamond's management that *day*.

I had two more stops to go before shooting for the episode wrapped. Next up was a trip to Powhatan Resort in historic Williamsburg, Virginia. The Powhatan was a legacy property, and with nearly eight hundred units, one of our largest and most popular worldwide. But precisely because it was big, I was curious to see how meticulously the staff would be able to care for every detail and project.

Greg, a mechanical engineer at this resort, had the will and the dedication but not the equipment or the support staff he needed to do his job properly. He and I sanded down a ceiling patch job in an unoccupied unit. What took an hour would have taken ten minutes with the proper tools. The Meaning of Yes is meant for our team members as much as for our customers. This came as a pointed reminder that my focus on one couldn't come at the expense of the other. The two were intertwined.

Finally, the end was in sight. We journeyed to my last stop at the Villa Mirage in Scottsdale, Arizona, where I was to work the front desk. I figured, "Easy enough."

It was anything but.

First, my photo—along with the Meaning of Yes pledge—was directly above the front desk. My palms were sweating; I assumed that this time I'd be ousted not on my terms, but on a guest's or a colleague's. For the first time during the entire shoot, I was glad to have such a shaggy wig that would cover not just my eyes but nearly my whole face.

My supervisor for the day was a young woman by the name of Amanda who couldn't have been more than twenty-some years old. She didn't miss a beat. She politely corrected my poor posture and told me *no* wasn't in my vocabulary—she not only acted the Meaning of Yes, but she recited it verbatim too. Not one to shy away from her opinions, Amanda chided that even some common hotel industry practices, like overbooking, had no place in Diamond Resorts' playbook. With this final encounter on the show, someone had succeeded in teaching me about the Meaning of Yes, an episode twist I did not see coming. I had genuinely learned from one of my youngest team members. For that, I was grateful.

When I flew home, I had plenty to reflect on. Walking into this unchartered *Undercover Boss* territory, I had assumed it would be up to me to model the behavior I expected from Diamond Resorts International team members. What I learned was that my job wasn't only to model the Meaning of Yes behavior, attitude, and outlook but to shine a spotlight on the incredible people already living this approach and celebrate their successes rather than my own.

## From Supervisor to Supporter

It's difficult to put into words exactly how much the *Undercover Boss* experience changed my way of thinking. The show producers wanted me to invite the four individuals I had worked most closely with during shooting back to Diamond Resorts headquarters, to sit in a conference room of some sort, as I revealed that they had really been working with the boss. In the past, the "undercover bosses" had donated $5,000 or so to a charity of the employee's choice.

It just seemed so . . . insufficient. How do you thank someone for broadening the way you look at your own business, something you built from the ground up after years of pouring so much heart, soul, and hard work into it?

I told Eli and Chris that I had something different up my sleeve. They were to invite each of the four colleagues I spent time with to my home—a more personal setting. And, to repay them for keeping me in the dark about our shooting schedule, I was going to keep the show's producers in the dark about how I was choosing to show my appreciation to my team members.

That last part felt good.

Greg, Randy, Amanda, and Sarah were still all buying the ruse that they would be advising me on whether to pursue a career change in hospitality when they walked through my front door. I'll never forget the look of surprise on their faces when they saw me, clean-shaven and sporting a proper haircut instead of a floppy wig, coming around the corner. You can't fake that sort of shock.

Because they each taught me something unique about my own business, I decided that I would return the favor personally as well.

Greg, the engineer at Powhatan, got a commitment from me that we'd be updating engineering tools company-wide and an assurance that our open positions would be filled in a timely manner so that our current staff didn't have to shoulder a load fit for a team. In addition, Greg had opened up to me about his passions (cooking) and his troubles (a beat-up car that guzzled gas, and in so doing, a disproportionate amount of his paycheck). He received a new industrial-size freezer, a subscription to a "meat of the month" club, and a new hybrid truck. Oh, and about that gas money: I extended a $20,000 bonus, no strings attached.

Sarah, the call center representative, first and foremost received an apology from me. I'm aware that my pursuit of perfection can be intense—and in the stress of the moment, her obvious lack of training sent me over the edge. So, Sarah received a commitment that I would personally return to Miami not just to train her but the entire call center. In return for her grace under fire, I offered her a well-deserved, all-expenses-paid trip to Hawaii to decompress, plus the peace of mind that came with knowing I'd be covering her outstanding college loans.

Amanda, the front desk agent who tore into our overbooking practices, was assured that we'd be changing not just our script but also our behavior company-wide when we ran into those rare circumstances. Imagine, one person, at one resort, not even twenty-five years old, directly changing corporate policy for the better. She had a dream of going to Ireland to work; I offered her a managerial position at our resort in Bodyke Village, in Clare County, Ireland. But she also confided in me that her family was struggling to pay her mother's multiple sclerosis medical bills. She'd have $50,000 wired to her bank account by the time she flew home, to use as she wished.

Finally, there was Randy, the Southern gentleman who had lost his livelihood in a business deal gone bad and was making ends meet working in maintenance at our Los Abrigados resort. The fact that I almost perished in a fire under his watch notwithstanding, Randy perhaps taught me the most about perseverance, fortitude, and the power of a positive attitude. Even with all that had gone on in his own life, Randy was still focused on taking care of our guests, first and foremost. If that isn't the embodiment of the Meaning of Yes, I don't know what is. Because he was beyond generous in taking care of others, I wanted to do my best to repay him in kind. I assumed his $150,000 mortgage and wrote him and his wife a check for $50,000. The lessons he taught me were invaluable—this is something I could do as a mere token of appreciation.

There is no substitute for experiencing your team members' roles, responsibilities, and work ethic firsthand. In the days, weeks, months, and years following my first episode, I received both criticism and praise for being "the most generous boss" in *Undercover Boss* history. But just as I understand that others may have given back in different ways, this is how I chose to show my sincere gratitude. Each of these gestures felt right and authentic to me. And I've always lived my life with a "what you see is what you get" mentality—TV being no exception.

---

**There is no substitute for experiencing your team members' roles, responsibilities, and work ethic firsthand.**

---

TV was uncharted territory for someone who's spent his entire life working behind the scenes, which amplified the *Undercover Boss* effect all the more. After the show, when I would travel to resorts—newly acquired properties like Cabo Azul or longtime offerings in the Diamond portfolio— my team members would be eager to teach me about how they applied the Meaning of Yes in their own ways, in their own styles. I went from being supervisor to supporter. That change in attitude and approach in turn would allow my people to feel freer and encourage them to propose changes operationally, procedurally, and culturally. It boosted the efficacy of our institutionalized intrapreneurism approach as team members all over the world saw people just like them—on prime-time television—effect meaningful, measurable change in our company.

The experience as a whole was such a success, both for our firm and the production studio, that producers Eli Holzman and Chris Carlson asked me to become the only boss in *Undercover Boss* history to return and feature in a second episode.

Perhaps I'll recount that filming experience, which was just as moving, in another book one day. But after meeting three more amazing team members, each with even more incredible stories than the last, what became clear to me was that one-time honorariums were not enough. I could do more. Diamond Resorts could do better.

With $1 million of my own money and a matching $1 million grant from the company, we created the Diamond Resorts International Foundation. This foundation to this day serves as a crisis fund, overseen by a rotating board of elected employees, to help any team member, anywhere, who needs assistance in a particular time of their life. It never would have been created without the lessons of the *Undercover Boss* experience.

It's the proudest achievement of Diamond Resorts' commitment to institutionalized intrapreneurism created yet.

### The Final Word

- If you hold to your values, your business will be more likely to appreciate in value.

- The Meaning of Yes is meant as much for team members as for our customers. Our focus on one can't be at the expense of the other. The two are intertwined.

- Our job isn't just to model the Meaning of Yes behavior, attitude, and outlook but to shine a spotlight on the incredible people who are already living this approach, and to celebrate their successes.

- There's no substitute for experiencing your team members' roles, responsibilities, and work ethic firsthand.

# Underneath the Tip of the Iceberg

I'd be remiss if I left any of my readers with the impression that intrapreneurism only comes in large, swift, bold strokes like renovating hotels or starring in a reality TV show. It's the rarity, not the rule, to innovate in front of the world with big publicity moments like *Undercover Boss*.

Equal to the impact of changing the deeded-week system to a points-based system and to overhauling the culture enveloping our sales team was the work that our guests, customers, and members never saw but fully benefited from.

I'm talking about IT and technology. (Don't let your eyes glaze over just yet.)

Today, *every* business is in the technology business. Diamond Resorts isn't only competing with the Hiltons, Starwoods, and Marriotts of the world—we're competing with Google, Amazon, and Microsoft for the software engineers and IT professionals who can help us create a streamlined, friendly, and intuitive experience for our guests.

And so are you.

> No matter what industry you're in, we're all competing for the same top-tier technology talent. Do you have a mission and a vision that will attract these professionals to your business over Google, Amazon, and the like?

When we first purchased Sunterra, it came with a legacy software infrastructure prone to breakdowns and plagued by interface issues. Because our data systems were kept in one siloed location, every time we faced a power outage (which was more often than you'd think) the entire system came crashing down. Guests couldn't book online. Hotels couldn't check guests in. Sales teams couldn't close a contract with a prospective owner.

It was an undeniable, categorical mess.

The case study of how our team went from turning chaos into a logical, organized system that's constant, finely tuned, and continuously improved can be used as an example road map for any systems turnaround.

## Step #1: Invest in Talent You Trust

We led a multimonth executive search for the right person to head our technology systems and IT needs. This person was going to be the strategic capital from which every other subsequent decision would stem. They had to have exactly the right experience: exemplary skills, a combination of on-the-ground know-how and industry-trend mastery, and cultural cohesion. We believed that talent over technology was a strategic decision and investment, and we needed someone who was right on paper and willing to dive headlong into a company turnaround situation without handholding, all while being expected to deliver tangible results. We didn't need someone adept at maintaining systems; we needed someone with the business courage and capability to build customized ones from the ground up.

> Talent over technology is a strategic decision and investment.

The search was painstaking and precise—it made the needle in the haystack analogy seem like an enjoyable pastime in comparison. But when we found our person, there wasn't time to hesitate. We made an offer that day, knowing that if we didn't, someone else soon would.

## Step #2: Stabilize

We see it all too often, whether it's a new football coach prematurely implementing new practices and plays before getting to know the strengths of the team, or a new department head enacting sweeping changes without fully understanding the current policies they have inherited: People leap before they look.

The very first act our chief information officer took was not to announce upcoming changes but to immerse himself in a full audit of our current IT operations. He had three reasons:

1. He planned to earn the trust, goodwill, and credibility of the department by listening to team members' concerns, recognizing their good work where recognition was due, and he wanted to coach them through current problems that he could help them fix.

2. He needed the time and space to fully understand our current systems, warts and all.

3. He wanted to understand how other departments—sales, marketing, reservations, insights, and strategy—all hoped to use the IT infrastructure in the future. The resulting strategy would be holistic, not narrow, in focus.

Fully equipped with an understanding of the current internal landscape, it was time to instill systemic discipline. Especially in turnaround situations, disorganization can lead to more havoc than you started with. New standards can't just be announced; success depends on how they're enforced.

Here's one of my favorite stories of the IT team's attention to detail: The initial changes at that time were small in scope (changing out old wires for new, organizing strewn cables, standardizing equipment) but enforced with military-style discipline. If a cable was out of place, our CIO would pull it straight from the jack—first warning, fix it the right way. If he came back and the cable was still improperly laid, he'd pull two more. And so on.

What was the purpose of this? His team learned quickly that consistency in all projects—seemingly insignificant or not—was not just expected, but inspected. The added accountability was prerequisite culture change that increased the odds of more sweeping and consequential decisions being met with consistency and success, not incidental error. In turnaround situations, it's about communicating what's expected before following up with feedback from project inspections.

## Step #3: Prioritize

Rome wasn't built in a day, and for that matter, neither was Diamond Resorts' IT infrastructure. (To give a sense of just how far out we planned, at the time of this writing, our team is still executing against the road map our CIO initially developed in 2008.) But while our team sees room for improvement, our customers see measurable enhancements in our work.

Technology is a tool that can help teams in any industry deliver hospitality—but never replace it.

The first priority set by our CIO was to move our data systems to a secure location that was insulated from power outages, and therefore avoid frustrating downtime that affected our resorts, reservations, and sales. Everything else could wait.

The second priority was to maximize the customer experience with the tools we had available. For example, imagine when you're being greeted at the check-in desk. You've been to this particular resort for the past five years in a row, and the attendant asks if this is your first time staying with them. The front desk attendant might have good intentions, but the produced effect tells guests they aren't appreciated. Our current technology had the ability to solve that small problem so that every check-in pulled up the proper customer history. If the guest had been here every year before, team members welcomed them back and thanked them for their loyalty; if it was their first visit, team members prepared a welcome packet to help acclimate guests to the grounds. That's technology not replacing hospitality but improving it.

The third priority involved thinking for the future. If growth meant acquiring new resorts, were we prepared to efficiently and effectively bring them online? What system improvements could we make to ensure that when opportunity presented itself, we wouldn't be hindered by technology limitations? Even with satisfaction gains, our technology department is in lockstep with our strategy team to ensure that we're prepared for any scenario, any change. Thinking for the future is about solving customer problems before they ever appear. We also did all this with the understanding that technology is a tool that can help teams deliver hospitality, not replace it.

Innovation comes in all forms, from all departments. Entrepreneurs with breakout ideas, missions, and visions all too often get stuck on the big impact, high-visibility changes that make a spectacular splash. But it's the unsung moments, from IT support to system changes, that sustain an organization. To maximize the little decisions that accumulate into make-or-break moments for your business, it's about investing in the right people, thoughtfully stabilizing your current circumstances, and prioritizing the change you want to see in the future. With a clearly articulated vision and set of values (in our case, the Meaning of Yes), you align sweeping announcements with minor adjustments to take you where you always wanted your organization to go.

If business leaders in any field are being honest with you, they'll admit that entrepreneurship gets the glory, but a commitment to continuous, never-complacent intrapreneurship gets results.

## The Final Word

- *Every* business is fighting for top talent. We're all competing with Google, Amazon, and Microsoft to create a streamlined, friendly, intuitive experience for our guests.

- Show your employees that consistency in everything isn't just expected but *inspected*.

- Technology is a tool to help deliver—not replace—authentic human hospitality.

- Invest in the right people, thoughtfully stabilize your current circumstances, and prioritize the change you want to see in the future.

# Growing the Pie

I find that too often, entrepreneurs in today's business environments focus *solely* on competition, on how to win market share from other players in their own line of work or industry. That's well and good; but concentrating exclusively on competitive advantage incorrectly assumes we live in a static, zero-sum landscape, that all gains and losses are absolute, when in truth, they're relative.

In Macroeconomics 101, students learn the pie theory. Grossly compressed, this theory is the idea that free-market economics contributes to growing the slice of everyone's pie, so we're all better off than simply redistributing the portions we already have. I think the economic pie analogy can be applied to businesses. Even as we're all fighting for market share, can we do more, together, to grow the market we share?

## Making Las Vegas . . . *Las Vegas*

Here's a bit of Las Vegas lore to bring the idea of expanding business opportunity for all to life.

The founding of Las Vegas itself dates to 1905, when the San Pedro, Los Angeles and Salt Lake Railroad plotted a midpoint between Salt Lake City and Los Angeles to connect the country's main rail networks. Five years later, according to census documents, Las Vegas had 945 residents, of which 40 percent of the adult males worked for the railroad. By 1920, the town had more than doubled in size to a bustling population of 2,304, of which, again, a full 54 percent of all adult males worked directly for the railroad.[1]

For the next ten years, that's all Las Vegas seemed destined to be: a company-dominated outpost that most people traveled through and rarely stayed in.

That wouldn't last for long. As American history would have it, the Great Depression—and the federal projects created in response to create jobs and stimulate growth—put Las Vegas on the national map. Construction began on the Boulder Dam (now known as the Hoover Dam) in 1931, bringing workers and their families in droves. Las Vegas became the central supply and entertainment hub for these men who were busy with construction during the day but looking for entertainment at night.

Casinos and showgirl venues opened up along the town's sole paved road, Fremont Street, to attract workers with money in their pockets. The completion of the dam in 1936 led to a flood of abundant, cheap hydroelectricity. Soon the area's first documented lighted sign went up promoting Fremont's "Glitter Gulch." It was far from the last. In 1941, El Rancho Vegas resort opened just outside city limits on a barren stretch of US 91. That lonely piece of highway would soon be flanked by a seemingly never-ending stream of hotel-casinos. Today we fondly call that stretch of road where El Rancho first broke ground the Strip.

Throughout the mob era, throughout World War II, Las Vegas gained both notoriety and acclaim as America's boomtown—and quite literally so, in one particular sense. In the 1950s, Las Vegas–area World War II magnesium plants and gunnery bases gave way to covert Nevadan Cold War sites, most infamously the Nevada Test Site. There, between the years 1951 and 1963, on the outskirts of the Mojave Deserve, the US government detonated more than one hundred nuclear bombs aboveground. In fact, guests so often spotted the unmistakable mushroom clouds from the hotels on the Strip that postcards heralded tourists' visits to Las Vegas as stops in the "Up and Atom City."[2]

It all fed into the budding Las Vegas fable.

More mom-and-pop casinos popped up along the Strip as the years went by, leaving dusty parking lots and blighted spaces between them. But it wasn't until the fateful Thanksgiving of 1966, when eccentric businessman Howard Hughes checked into the penthouse of the Desert Inn (and never left), that Las Vegas entered the opulent, nightlife orbit we know it for today. (After facing eviction to make room for New Year's revelers, Hughes opted to buy the hotel outright, rather than move.) Hughes proceeded to gobble up more Las Vegas hotels—upward of $300 million worth—harbingering an era in which corporate conglomerates uprooted an entrenched mob presence. And they all concentrated in one area: the Strip.

## RE-CREATING THE LAS VEGAS STRIP

When you think of the Strip today, what comes to mind? Neon lights, mega casinos, and, of course, the iconic palm trees towering from the roadway median.

It wasn't always that way.

What was once a four-mile strip of dirt, rock, and oleanders became a scenic stretch of illuminated palm trees, shrubs, and grass stretching from Hacienda to Sahara Avenues. But why? Because the fiercely competitive casinos, restaurants, and hotels of Las Vegas realized they could do more to collectively enhance their growth opportunities together. And they did it by making the city a more glamorous, idyllic vacation destination *across the board.*

## The fiercely competitive casinos, restaurants, and hotels of Las Vegas realized they could do more to collectively enhance their growth opportunities together.

After opening Polo Towers and talking with others in Las Vegas (like Steve Wynn, who had opened the Mirage in 1989), it dawned on me that we could build the most beautiful, exquisite interiors to impress our guests; but customers' first impressions of our individual businesses were actually of Las Vegas as a whole. Back in the early 1990s, Las Vegas still felt like a patchwork of properties, rather than a unified, seamless experience in and of itself.

It was clear that to attract more tourists to Las Vegas—to grow our tourism pie—we'd have to care for the spaces between our competing properties.

In 1993, I was still the new kid on the Las Vegas block, but I made a name for myself by spending my afternoons going door-to-door collecting signatures of casino owners and managers. The goal was to create a petition of intent for the streetscaping design, which, ultimately, more than two hundred Strip–frontage property owners *unanimously* approved. That momentum turned into a consortium of more than one hundred committed Strip property owners who would *pay* for the streetscaping redesign construction and maintenance of a major Strip beautification project. The deal hinged on a provision that, although the local government of Clark County would manage the new median, the project wouldn't cost taxpayers a dime. *Not a single cent.*

When I look at Las Vegas, perhaps the most competitive city on earth, I see physical proof of what corporate collaborations can accomplish. It took two years of construction and cost those hundred Strip property owners $13 million to fund, but by 1995, the Las Vegas Boulevard Beautification Project proved an amazing success. The median—the Strip's collective sinew—was now lush with seventy thousand plants and shrubs (including fourteen

The Las Vegas Strip Renderings,
before and after.
(Photos by Eric Figge.)

hundred palm trees), all managed by a state-of-the-art computer-controlled lighting and irrigation system.[3]

When you stepped out of a resort or casino on the Strip, the Las Vegas experience didn't end—rather, it unfurled before you.

---

## When I look at Las Vegas, perhaps the most competitive city on earth, I see physical proof of what corporate collaborations can accomplish.

---

Today, the Strip is an international icon. It's designated as a Nevada Scenic Byway, thanks, in part, to that four and a half miles of artistic streetscaping only competitive collaboration could produce.[4] Perhaps it's impossible to quantify in market terms exactly what the Las Vegas Boulevard Beautification Project contributed to the city. But we do know this: In 1995, fewer than thirty million people visited Las Vegas; in 2016, that number well surpassed forty-two million.

So, you tell me: Where does strategic competition end and collaboration begin?[5]

### The Final Word

- Even as we're all fighting for market share, can we do more together to grow the market we share?
- Corporate collaborations represent another approach to strategic growth that can complement corporate competitions.
- Strategic collaborations can accomplish amazing things.

# Brand USA

The experience and success of working to orchestrate the Las Vegas Boulevard Beautification Project may have faded from view as I concentrated on growing the Diamond Resorts International name and brand, but it was never far from my mind.

That's why I paid attention when Robert Brady, the US Representative for Pennsylvania's First Congressional District, introduced a specific piece of legislation in the House by the name of the Travel Promotion Act of 2009. Not exactly a title that speaks to the imagination or rolls off the tongue, but the program it stood for was truly exciting.

The bill set out to create a nonprofit organization with the twofold task of (1) better communicating US entry policies to international travelers and (2) promoting leisure, business, and scholarly travel to the United States.

First, I thought: "It's about time."

Second, a split second later, I said: "I want to be a part of this."

## The Need to Market US Destinations

Up until this point, regions, states, and municipalities all competed for tourism dollars by setting up their own individual and competing marketing organizations. There was no single, overarching umbrella organization that promoted the United States as a destination for foreign travel.

Think about that for a moment: Whereas other countries—from the UK to India, from France to Brazil, from Australia to Iceland—had dedicated ministers of tourism actively and aggressively promoting their countries to capture global travelers' dollars, we were silently standing still. That meant Las Vegas, Florida, New York City, Illinois—any region or city that so chose— was left to its own devices, consequently advertising without direction or alignment to Europe, Asia, and every country in between. No coordination, no overarching strategy—just little American destination principalities duking it out for inbound travelers.

Not only was it clumsy, but the result was also confusing and incredibly cost-ineffective.

Consider the following independently verified assessment of what the US travel industry came to know as the Lost Decade, a period stretching from 2000 to 2009:

> Outside the United States, international travel has experienced explosive growth over the last decade and has been a leading contributor to job creation and economic growth worldwide. [But] the failure of the United States during this decade to simply keep pace with the growth in international long-haul travel worldwide has cost our economy millions of lost visitors and billions in lost spending that would have supported hundreds of thousands of U.S. jobs and generated billions in tax revenue.[1]

From 2000 to 2009, the number of overseas travelers visiting the United States fell by a full 9 percent. In that same time period, international tourist arrivals worldwide actually *grew* to 880 million in 2009, up by nearly 200 million since 2000.[2]

In real market dollars, here's what this 9 percent drop cost the United States economy, according to a report by the U.S. Travel Association:[3]

- 68.3 million lost visitors, each of whom on average spends well over $4,000

- $509 billion in lost spending, including $214 billion in direct spending and $295 billion in downstream spending at restaurants, clothing retailers, and scores of other small businesses

- 441,000 lost jobs, direct and indirect, in all regions of the country

- $270 billion in direct lost trade surplus, as international travel is the United States' largest service export

- $32 billion in direct lost tax revenue at the federal, state, and local levels

With numbers as colossal as these slipping through America's fingers, and with such a far reach, there's no doubt you and your household were fiscally affected by this "lost decade" of American travel. The question is not *if* but rather *by how much*.

---

## 68.3 M
**Number of "lost visitors" to the US between 2000 and 2009**

The failure of the United States over the first decade of the new millennium to simply keep pace with the growth of international long-haul travel has resulted in the loss of 68.3 million potential visitors.

---

## 606 B
**Amount of "lost spending" between 2000 and 2010**

The loss of 78 million visitors cost our economy $606 billion in lost spending.

---

## 467 K
**Number of "lost jobs" between 2001 and 2010**

The resulting lost spending has cost our economy 467,000 potential jobs.

---

(Citation: US Travel Association)

# 441,000 LOST US TRAVEL-RELATED JOBS
# ACROSS ALL SECTORS OF THE ECONOMY

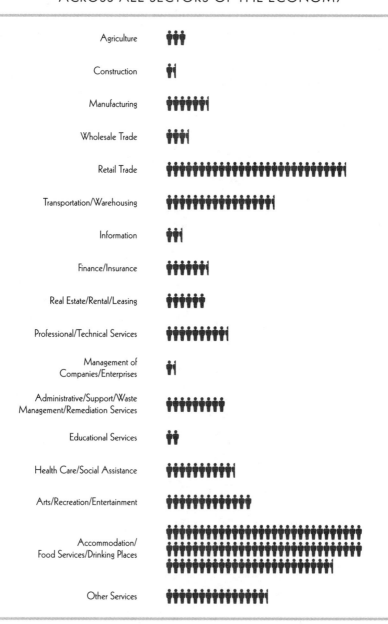

2,000 Lost Jobs  =  👤          (Citation: US Travel Association)

## TOP 10 COUNTRIES' MARKETING BUDGETS, COMPARED TO THE UNITED STATES

| NATION | PROMOTIONAL SPENDING in Millions (2005) |
|---|---|
| Greece | $151.4 |
| Mexico | $149.2 |
| Malaysia | $117.9 |
| Australia | $113.3 |
| U.K. | $89.2 |
| Turkey | $80.0 |
| France | $63.3 |
| Italy | $61.9 |
| China | $60.0 |
| Canada | $58.5 |
| U.S. | $0.0 |

(Citation: UNWTO)

## Initial Resistance

Despite the wealth of evidence supporting the need for a nationally coordinated program to market US destinations to world travelers, the Travel Promotion Act faced resistance from staunch Republicans once it entered the Senate. Two in particular, Senators Jim DeMint (R-SC) and Tom

Coburn (R-OK), argued that these marketing endeavors should be left to the private sphere on principle.[4] Their thinking went something like this: A public-private partnership to boost tourism flirted with "corporate welfare," and secondarily, with the popularity of American music, TV, and movies, who didn't know about the United States, anyway?

I later learned of a conversation between Roger Dow, an incredible advocate for the Travel Promotion Act as president and CEO of the U.S. Travel Association (and a man I would later count as a close friend), and a certain member of Congress. When discussing the merits of the legislation, the congressperson concluded that they wouldn't vote for this bill because it was "extraneous," given America's reputation in the world. Dow, a gentleman through and through, demurred and asked how long the congressperson had been in office.

"Oh, twenty or something years by now." To which Dow coyly replied, "Well, you must not even need to campaign anymore; given your reputation, everyone in your district must know you by now!"

The member of Congress said that to the contrary, millions and millions of dollars poured into their election from outside the state every term without fail, they held one of the most hotly contested seats, and even after twenty years in office, they won the last challenge by the skin of their teeth.

When Roger pointed out the connection—that we can't rest on reputation alone in the face of active and aggressive promotion from countries abroad—the congressperson signaled an end to the discussion by saying, "That's just different."

This one member aside, a majority of both chambers of Congress grew to understand the negative implications of the United States being one of the last industrialized countries in the world without a nationally coordinated program to promote its destinations to international travelers. As lawmakers began to come to grips with the rippling economic costs, the bill earned both steam and bipartisan support. Among the most fervent champions of the Travel Promotion Act were Representatives Bill Delahunt (D-MA), Roy Blunt (R-MO), and Sam Farr (D-CA) and Senators Byron Dorgan (D-ND),

John Ensign (R-NV), Daniel Inouye (D-HI), Amy Klobuchar (D-MN), and my personal friend, Harry Reid (D-NV).

At the time, Senator Reid and I talked regularly as the legislation inched closer and closer to a vote. Representing Nevada, he intuitively understood the transformative power of tourism on a city, an industry, and an economy writ large. What we both wanted was an opportunity not only to better the state's market share of the current inbound travel business but also the chance to bake a bigger slice for everyone.

## A Public/Private Partnership

When President Obama signed the Travel Promotion Act into law on Thursday, March 4, 2010, Senator Reid and I saw it as an historic moment. Oxford Economics, an independent and expert economic forecasting firm, estimated that a successful national promotion would yield $4 billion in new spending annually, create forty thousand new jobs, and generate $321 million in new tax revenue each year. The Congressional Budget Office reported that the Travel Promotion Act would reduce the federal deficit by $425 million over ten years.

Senator Reid and I both believed that this innovative public-private partnership combining the accountability of government with the expertise of business could accomplish even more.

Here's how it was all slated to work: The law created the nonprofit Corporation for Travel Promotion (the name was even clunkier than the title of the bill itself), designed to promote the United States as a travel destination and explain travel and security policies to international visitors.

A ten-dollar fee would now be charged to visitors from countries included in the Visa Waiver Program (VWP), which would partially fund the public-private organization. These visitors would pay the fee every two years when they registered online using the Department of Homeland Security's Electronic System for Travel Authorization.

These fees, combined with private donations, would fund the nonprofit's marketing campaigns to bring visitors to the United States and efforts to educate potential travelers on entry requirements and processes. Up to 20 percent of the private donations could be received in cash, and the remaining 80 percent would be classified as in-kind support.

The funds received from the fees on VWP travelers would be drawn on to match these private donations, up to $100 million a year. In 2012, every dollar of cash or in-kind support received by the nonprofit would be matched with two dollars of Electronic System for Travel Association funds held by the US Treasury. In every subsequent year, private funds would be matched one-to-one.

And here's the kicker: Any money raised from the VWP over $100 million a year would go *straight* to deficit reduction.

The bottom line, according to Roger Dow: The nonprofit Corporation for Travel Promotion wouldn't cost taxpayers a cent while creating a new lever "to serve as an economic stimulant, job generator, and diplomatic tool,"[5] which meant, if the corporation was able to raise the projected $200 million annually, the American organization would be the largest national tourism communications program in the world.

## Forming the Board

With stakes and hopes high, the United States Department of Commerce immediately began the search to fill the eleven positions on the corporation's voluntary board with representatives from all corners of the US travel industry.

(The law *specifically* called for the board to be comprised of individuals with expertise and experience in the following ten sectors: (1) hotels; (2) restaurants; (3) small businesses; (4) travel distribution services; (5) attractions and recreations; (6) city conventions or visitors bureaus; (7) state tourism offices; (8) airlines; (9) immigration laws and policies; and (10) passenger railroads.)

Nearly seven months after the bill's signing in the White House Rose Garden, Secretary of Commerce Gary Locke announced the Corporation for Travel Promotion's board of directors for the first time. Roger Dow, who for the entire duration between the bill's passage and the board's announcement had been working on strategic suggestions, frameworks, and planning, listened intently to the reading of the list:

- Caroline Beteta, president and CEO; California Travel and Tourism Commission; Sacramento, California

- George Fertitta, CEO; NYC & Company; New York, New York

- Daniel J. Halpern, president and CEO; Jackmont Hospitality Inc.; Atlanta, Georgia

- Tom Klein, president; Sabre Holdings; Southlake, Texas

- David Lim, chief marketing officer; Amtrak; Washington, DC

- Mark Schwab, senior vice president, alliances, international and regulatory affairs; United Airlines; Chicago, Illinois

- Diane Shober, tourism director; State of Wyoming; Cheyenne, Wyoming

- Al Weiss, president, worldwide operations; Walt Disney Parks and Resorts; Orlando, Florida

- Roy Yamaguchi, owner and founder; Roy's Restaurant; Newport Beach, California

- Lynda S. Zengerle, partner; Steptoe & Johnson LLP; Washington, DC

- Stephen Cloobeck, chairman and CEO; Diamond Resorts International; Las Vegas, Nevada

Dow's response: *"Cloo-Who?!"*

An industry man, Roger knew everyone announced to the board and knew them well—except for me. My association was with timeshare, after all, not just standard hotels. We agreed to meet in New York City at a bar the following Tuesday simply to introduce ourselves. When the time came, we actually had to email one another to "stand up" so we could recognize and find each other in the crowded lounge.

We decided then and there that if we really wanted this venture to be successful, we didn't have the luxury of waiting for the Department of Commerce to dole out marching orders. (Given that it took them seven months to announce a board, we teased that the law's purview would expire if we waited for them to set the date for the first meeting.) We'd have to take the initiative and onus on creating the plans ourselves. And that's what we did. We scheduled a first informal full board meeting about two weeks later, in Washington, DC, so every member could attend.

## Getting to Work

Not one to squander an opportunity or a moment's time, through my own volition I funded and opened a bank account of $50,000 operating cash for the Corporation, took out directors and officers insurance on myself and the ten other board members, and had my lawyer craft an initial draft of managerial bylaws to use as a working document.

At the morning meeting a few days later, I introduced myself to the group and proceeded to nominate myself as chairman, calling to the fore the steps I had already taken and asking if there were any objections. With that, I was elected, and we got to work. I believe that if you want an opportunity, asking for it is necessary but not sufficient; you need to demonstrate why you're the right person for it.

By then, the pleasantries were over. I wanted this organization to prove itself right out of the gate. But with ten diverse and distinct interests represented on the board, harmony was never the objective. Collaboration can actually sometimes be harder than competition. We learned that lesson early in our search for a CEO who would oversee the day-to-day operations of the organization. I delegated a search committee that came back with a recommendation that astounded me.

To run an American outfit promoting tourism, they wanted to hire . . . a Brit.

Did this individual have the right sort of experience and background? Yes. But could you imagine the backlash from the press—and more important, the industry—if we told them there was no American professional qualified to run the Corporation for Travel Promotion? Insult was only added to injury when this person asked for a salary substantially more than $400,000 (the income of the president of the United States) and wanted to run a US government public-private partnership not in DC, but in Boston.

None of it squared.

Ultimately we went in a different—and I would argue more appropriate—direction. But this executive search created a real rift within the board that would rear its head later.

## Setting Goals

For now, we pressed on. With little direction from the Department of Commerce, we began the hard work of mapping exactly how we'd operate and setting ambitious but realistic goals.

Our five core principles became:

1. **Creative innovative marketing:** To promote the entirety of the United States, to, through, and beyond the gateways

2. **Market the "Welcome":** Inspire, inform, welcome, and thank travelers while accurately communicating vital and compelling information about visa and entry policies

3. **Build and maintain trust:** Focus on inclusive, proactive, and transparent outreach through integrity with key stakeholders worldwide through words, actions, and results

4. **Add and create value:** Pioneer cooperative marketing platforms and programs that leverage and grow the USA brand in ways our partners would be challenged or unable to do on their own

5. **Drive results:** Maximize return on investment by sending the right messages through the right channels, in the right markets, at the right times, and with the right investment levels

But before turning over the creative reins so that the organization's staff could develop our country's first unified marketing campaign, which we slated to launch in the spring of 2012, I had one sticking point.

We had to do something about our *awful* name.

## A New Name

In November 2011, the Corporation for Travel Promotion became Brand USA. With the change, everyone who encountered our organization for the first time knew exactly what we stood for, exactly what we were focused on, and exactly what we were promoting.

Our corresponding new logo was created to be fresh, welcoming, and inclusive, seeking to remind the world that the "United States of Awesome Possibilities" welcomes everyone. It featured a collection of pixel dots joined together to form the letters *USA*. But on closer inspection, each of the dots individually showcased different tableaus of the diverse colors, people, and destinations across America. The name and representation together purposefully emphasized the boundless possibilities of the United States.

## Introducing Hospitality

With the marketing staff in place and strategic planning under way, I turned my attention to what many considered the intractable problems with the inbound traveler entry process. That meant dealing directly with US Customs and Border Protection (CBP).

As you may know, the sixty thousand employees of the CBP are charged with a single mission: to uphold the country's national security and prevent terrorists and weapons from crossing our borders, all while facilitating lawful international travel and trade.

On any given day, the CBP screens more than sixty-seven thousand cargo containers, arrests more than eleven hundred individuals, and seizes nearly six tons of illicit drugs.

Coming from the hospitality world, my stepping into the world of law enforcement was no less than a clash of cultures. I knew my place wasn't to adjust procedure—the CBP enforces hundreds and hundreds of US laws and regulations—but perhaps to remind the CBP that the full definition of security wasn't only physical but also economic; that protecting safety didn't necessarily have to come at the expense of economic health and viability.

Knowing that the CBP processes a million visitors to the United States every single day, I had two goals: (1) that CBP enforcement would say, "Welcome to the United States" to each and every traveler who presented their passports for inspection; and (2) that upon conducting their due diligence, these same professionals would wish every single legitimate traveler, "Enjoy your stay."

That's it. A greeting and a closing. But introducing just this symbolic gesture of hospitality into a customs and police organization would take dozens of trainings and years to implement.

I knew this sort of attitudinal change wouldn't come at the behest of an outsider; it needed the support from the very top of the organization. I found an ally in CBP Deputy Executive Assistant Commissioner John Wagner.

By 2008, Wagner had already taken it on himself to launch two groundbreaking programs that fundamentally changed more than a century-old arrival process for returning Americans and foreign visitors. He recognized intuitively that long wait times combined with a hostile customs and immigrations atmosphere wouldn't engender support for heightened, necessary security at airports; it would only create festering problems across every safety measure, from the most technical procedures down to the simplest commonsense steps.

As if that alone wasn't impressive enough, Wagner was a driving force behind the Global Entry Trusted Traveler program. This program has enrolled more than two million people to date and emerged as a fixture in approximately fifty US airports. Global travelers attributed the program to shortening lengthy, headache-inducing lines so that the lines took just minutes.

I needed to align Brand USA with someone with that sort of innovative thinking and vision.

There was skepticism at first, and there were plenty of debates. For instance, should a CBP officer have to smile while enforcing a potentially dangerous security mission? The Meaning of Yes mind-set would take that for granted, but the CBP recoiled at the idea. And as important as hospitality is to me, they were right. Our intent was never to ask customs and immigrations officials to be Brand USA ambassadors first and officers second, but to simply remember that they served as a de facto introduction to the United States for legitimate international visitors and the de facto "welcome home" to Americans returning stateside. There was middle ground we could all agree on: leaving behind an aura of intimidation for one of efficient professionalism.

Wagner and the CBP eventually mandated my two asks—the greeting and the good wishes—but there was a critical window we had to seize to ensure it truly took root. I traveled with Wagner as he tested different airports' adoption of the new arrival procedures personally. He was visible and out in front of his people, championing and explaining the importance of these greetings. It wasn't just a procedural change, another memo to be disregarded; this was a *behavioral* shift to which everyone was held accountable.

This was Wagner's version of putting his business card on every front desk.

It's impossible to quantify the impact of the greeting and good wishes, but if you've ever traveled internationally, you've certainly felt the difference between a welcoming arrivals process and an arduous one. And for their part, CBP officers dealt with less agitated and better informed and prepared travelers, which made their jobs more efficient and effective.

It was a true win-win collaboration, one that led to even more partnership opportunities. I've found that collaborations are more than opportunities to cooperate with partners; they're opportunities to learn from partners.

## MAKING A BETTER EXPERIENCE

Cloobeck, Dow, Wagner: You'll be forgiven if these names didn't ring any bells. But you won't catch any slack for this next one: Among Brand USA's founding fourteen partners was no less than the Walt Disney Company itself. And while Disney is known first and foremost for its stories and characters beloved across generations, it also had expertise in another arena directly compatible with our mission of making customs and immigrations a better experience for everyone: queue science.

Through its theme parks division, Disney mastered the art of organizing, directing, and moving large volumes of people while minimizing the irritation you'd expect from someone asked to wait in line (often for a long time). Disney engineers showed Wagner and his team how the same wait could feel drastically different, given different approaches to queuing. Did you sort people into one long line? Twenty shorter ones? Ten lines that later fed into one?

To distill hours and hours of conversation and a rich subject of scientific study into one broad takeaway for Wagner's team: The more ports of entry that could keep people moving, however incrementally, the less likely they'd be to focus on the overall amount of time spent waiting. Think Einstein's theory of relativity: People moving at different speeds perceive time itself differently. Translated for our purposes, forty-five minutes spent inching forward is a far better experience than forty-five minutes spent standing still.

To cap their partnership, Disney donated a short-form documentary video for the CBP to play in international arrival halls. Called *Welcome: Portraits of America*, the seven-minute video didn't focus on traditional sightseeing destinations but rather featured Americans from diverse regions and all walks of life. It was played for months in the arrival halls at over twenty US airports.

## The Measure of Success

During this time working side-by-side with the CBP to improve the traveler experience entering the United States, I got a phone call from one of the board members. Some of them still felt slighted that I had overturned their CEO search process and also felt that I was pushing too fast and too far in making Brand USA changes. They told me they had the votes to depose me as chairman of the board, and they told me they were calling a meeting.

> **In strategic collaborations, harmony is not the most important measure of success; efficacy is.**

I distinctly remember taking a moment to let this news soak in. I make no pretense that my style can be gruff and that I prioritize results over an easy approach. But I thought we were all on the same page that this work *mattered*. I thought we agreed it deserved nothing but the utmost attention and urgency. With Brand USA, we were fighting for international tourism dollars, economic growth, and job creation here at home. It was our duty to move fast and to start winning back the ground we had lost over the last ten years. What had I missed?

The silence on the other end of the phone, waiting for my reply, hung heavy in the air. "By chance, did you ever read the bylaws I drafted? The ones the board agreed to. The ones you signed?" I intoned. In the bylaws, I had inserted a clause that stated only the chairman of the board had the executive authority to call meetings. And what did this contingent of the board need to vote on my chairmanship? That's right. An official meeting.

I didn't relish the animosity on the board, but my mission was never to make friends, to rub elbows, to network. No, my mission was to get to work. I know also that in strategic collaborations, harmony is not the most important measure of success; efficacy is.

## SETTING UP FOR LONG-TERM SUCCESS

I finished out the last few months of my two-year position. And I'm proud to say that in this time, the board set up Brand USA for long-term success. Before I left, I had the opportunity to meet with President Obama in the Oval Office to share with him the importance and efficacy of our activities to date.

Here's what I was able to share with him.

Brand USA reduced wait times for US tourist visas from an average of 130 days to 105 days, shaving off nearly a full month. When international tourists arrived in the States, they arrived better informed, better prepared, and dealt with a better CBP security system in major airport hubs across the United States. Therefore, our work directly enhanced America's standing and reputation in the world.

Brand USA hit its $100 million revenue-raising target each and every year, subsequently contributing millions of dollars directly to deficit reduction. Every dollar in marketing spent by Brand USA generated a $47 return on investment.[6] In plainer terms, every marketing dollar spent by Brand USA translated to $47 injected into the US economy.

And finally, this meant Brand USA's inaugural efforts amounted to $3.4 billion in additional visitor spend, generating $7.4 billion in business sales, $3.8 billion in gross domestic product, $2.2 billion in personal income, and fifty-three thousand jobs.[7]

● ● ●

Brand USA is still operating today, committed to growing international travel to the United States, an industry that currently supports 1.8 million American jobs, and benefits virtually every sector of the US economy. It counts over seven hundred private and public organizations as partners, streamlining efforts to invite the entire world to explore the incredible, incomparable, and truly limitless destinations and experiences the United States has to offer.

The organization represents what's possible when traditional competitors raise their heads above the parapet to look for opportunities, to do more than just challenge one another, to grow alongside each other. When we expand markets, rather than just fight for oxygen within them, we find more often than not there's room for new entrants, established players, and everyone in between.

## The Final Word

- If you want a position or role, don't just ask for it; demonstrate why you're the right person for it.

- Collaborations are more than opportunities to cooperate with partners; they're opportunities to *learn* from partners.

- Harmony isn't always the most important measure of success; efficacy is.

# PART FOUR

# We're All in Hospitality Now

After years at the helm of Diamond Resorts, I stepped down from the organization I built, took public, and grew into one of the most successful timeshare companies in the world. To pass the torch to the next generation's capable hands was one of the more wrenching yet rewarding decisions I ever made. Having globe-trotted the world nonstop for years, it was time to pause, reflect, take stock of, and consider what I still had left to do in my "next" career, whatever that might prove to be.

Suffice it to say, much in the business world has changed since I started developing commercial shopping malls decades ago. Companies have come and gone, industries have risen and fallen, new inventions have changed not just the course of commerce but daily life (and even the future we anticipate).

There's also been a dark side to the way business has evolved: companies taking more than they should and not being transparent with stakeholders, stockholders, and customers. I'll let you draw on the cases that come to mind—there are offenders in nearly every industry.

But above all else, here is what I ask you to remember: Absolutely no social contract, doctrine, or phenomenon has done more to help more people in more places improve their quality of life than free-market capitalism. It is incontrovertibly the greatest societal structure that's afforded billions across the world, and millions of Americans, the opportunity to find meaning for themselves by creating value for others.

Consider, in broad strokes, the change the Western world has seen since adopting free-market capitalism between 1750 and the early 1800s according to Mackey and Sisodia[1]:

- Two centuries ago, more than 85 percent of the world's population lived in extreme poverty (earning less than $1 per day); that number is now about 15 percent.

- Adjusting for affordability and quality improvements, the standard living of ordinary Americans since 1800 has increased 10,000 percent—a number that's difficult to fathom, let alone truly appreciate.

- More than half of the world's population now lives in countries with democratic governments elected by universal suffrage. Compare that to zero people just 120 years ago, as our own democracy and others denied women or minorities or both the right to vote.

- Finally, free-market economies report a higher level of life satisfaction. The top quartile of economically free countries has a life satisfaction index of 7.5 out of 10, compared with 4.7 for the bottom quartile. The self-determination associated with free markets, business opportunities, and economic mobility leads to greater prosperity and greater happiness.

There are many other statistics that all point to the same conclusion: Business has been an overwhelming force for good and for progress. Many of the daily conveniences we so often take for granted have been made possible only because inventors, innovators, and entrepreneurs took a bold chance on themselves and their ideas by bringing them to market.

But what's done more to advance collective interests in the past two hundred years won't be sufficient to move us forward into the next twenty. Businesses today are forced to contend with a public that's been awakened to the truth that economics aren't separated from ethics; they're integrated. There's no such thing as "it's just business." There are always human costs and human opportunities at stake.

> The businesses best poised for long-term success understand that economics and enterprise aren't separated from ethics; they're integrated.

My friend Mike Milken epitomizes this point. For those who don't know Milken, let me introduce him with all humility by saying perhaps no one in my generation has done more to revolutionize the capital markets, making them more efficient, dynamic, and democratic. He's left an indelible legacy as a pioneer for finding new ways to get more capital to more businesses—thousands of them—thus creating millions of jobs over time.

How? With a clear intention to finance business with the potential to change the world.

The financial theories he developed, executed, and proved in the markets did exactly that.

## Mike Milken

Milken went to the University of California, Berkeley, with a mind to study science. He had grown up watching the space program lift people's sights to a brighter future, embolden their ideas of what could be possible if we set our collective efforts and energy to it. He wanted to be part of this American quest.

That all changed in the summer of 1965, when Milken, living in Los Angeles, experienced the visceral unrest of the Watts Riots firsthand. The seminal moment came when an African American man explained that these weren't his factories burning down, nor were they his community's. The man told Mike matter-of-factly that he had no way of getting the capital he needed to own much of anything. That meant his prospects of pursuing his dreams were severely limited.

This is someone who could see the American dream but who couldn't access it.

Perhaps Mike's best chance of addressing the biggest challenges of the day wasn't through staring at the stars but taking a hard look at the societal problems in his own backyard.

That fall semester, Mike promptly changed his major to business.

Over the course of his freshly redirected studies, a set of ideas about society, finance, and prosperity began to coalesce in Mike's mind. It occurred to him that three types of assets—human capital, social capital, and financial capital—were much more closely related than most people realized. Without social capital (schools, for example), human capital can't develop. And without human capital (people's skills), financial capital can't be deployed productively. Mike connected these ideas in a way that had never been so clearly expressed before.

$$P = \Sigma Ft_i * (\Sigma HC_i + \Sigma SC_i + \Sigma RA_i)$$

| Financial Technology | Human Capital | Social Capital | Real Assets |
|---|---|---|---|
| The Innovative processes & components including: | Productivity: | • Rule of law | • Cash |
| • Convertible bonds | • Skills | • Property rights | • Receivables |
| • Preferred stock | • Education | • Public health | • Real estate |
| • High-yield bonds | • Training | • Universal education | • Factories |
| • Collateralized loans | • Experience | • Religious freedom | • Capital equiptment |
| • Collateralized bonds | • Creativity | • Police/fire protection | • Roads |
| • Equity-linked securities | • Habits | • Cultural resources | • Buildings |
| • Securitized obligations (mortgages, credit cards, etc.) | • Values | • Universal suffrage | • Infrastructure |
| • Derivatives | | • Protection of creditors | |
| | | • Rigorous financial reporting standards | |
| | | • Transparent markets | |
| | | • Regulatory continuity | |

More than forty years ago, as a student at Berkeley and then Wharton, Mike Milken developed a formula for prosperity that applies in any economic cycle.

Mike Milken's formula[2] covers:

- **Financial technology**—which refers to new processes and organizational forms, innovative types of securities, and derivatives of securities. At the risk of dating Mike, almost no financial technology existed when he was a student.

- **Human capital**—includes the collective abilities, training, and experience of people. It's the most valuable resource on earth.

- **Social capital**—includes universal education and health care, police and fire protection, religious freedom, a sense of neighborhood bonds, and widely available cultural resources. But it also includes the incentives for risk taking inherent in established property rights, protection of creditors, regulatory continuity, transparent markets, and rigorous financial reporting standards.

- **Real assets**—include cash, receivables, real estate, factories, capital equipment, and anything else that can be assigned a specific current value.

In short, stable economic growth is most likely in societies where everyone has access to education, can participate in the political process, and can aspire to ownership of property. Mike's formula led to millions of people, institutions, and entire countries thinking about finance in a larger context by clarifying the true value of a business (or, for that matter, of a household, government, or a country) as not fully reflected only in the numbers, which ignore human and social capital.

Here's why this matters, not just to me, but to entrepreneurs and business leaders everywhere: Mike's studies at Berkeley showed that access to financial capital—the lifeblood of any business—historically had been severely restricted. As late as the 1960s, a small number of bankers controlled it and doled it out to privileged clients, the several hundred corporations that boasted an "investment-grade" rating. As one of the most regulated industries in the nation, banks were encouraged and predisposed to provide loans only to "safe" borrowers and their managements, who almost invariably were male, white, and "established."

The result? The routine denial of capital to entrepreneurs with great business ideas but no establishment credentials. Among its many victims were minorities, blue-collar workers, and women. Because access to capital wasn't truly democratic, neither was prosperity. That meant untold numbers of missed growth opportunities for individuals, families, and American society as a whole.

It didn't have to be that way.

Mike, not just brilliant but determined to make a difference, would use this theory, which valued human capital alongside real assets, in parallel with his underlying and unyielding commitment to social change to finance entrepreneurs who had visions for great companies but little access to typical bank financing. With Milken's financial backing, these entrepreneurs unleashed economic engines and drivers of mass employment.

Among the many, many visionaries Mike Milken would back were Bill McGowan (MCI, telecommunications), Ted Turner (Turner Broadcasting, cable television), Craig McCaw (McCaw Cellular, mobile telephones), Steve Wynn (Wynn Resorts, luxury hotels), Leonard Riggio (Barnes & Noble, book retailing), Bob Toll (Toll Brothers, homebuilding), John Malone (TCI/Liberty Media, cable network), Steve Ross (Time-Warner, cable television), Dr. Armand Hammer and Dr. Ray Irani (Occidental Petroleum), Mel Simon (Simon Property Group, shopping malls), Calvin Klein (Calvin Klein Inc., fashion house), and . . . *me*.

Milken mentored me for years, which prepared me to navigate the financial nuances of the Sunterra purchase in 2007—in no small way making possible all that Diamond Resorts has and will continue to achieve.

Milken, one of the most successful financial minds in modern times, got what he wanted by giving others—people like me—what we needed: a chance.

I could write another book on Milken's experiences, expertise, and accomplishments, but instead, let me suggest a simple understanding of Milken's contributions. Namely, that his success hinged not on merely being a brilliant mind (though he most assuredly is) but because he applied basic principles of *hospitality*—the art of understanding people, caring for the details others don't, and, most important of all, valuing meritocracy over hierarchy—and applied those principles to the field of finance.

By factoring human considerations into economic science, Milken developed financial innovations that powered job growth in America for a quarter century.

And Milken's experiences and accomplishments show us what's to be gained in applying the principles of hospitality to arenas, businesses, and industries where it's traditionally been undervalued or ignored outright.

## Looking Ahead

But what about the next quarter century? What will fuel meaningful and measurable job growth when computers and machines outpace traditional commerce and manufacturing?

There's no doubt in my mind that a certain kind of business will be better poised for success in the next ten, twenty, and two hundred years—and those are businesses that don't just service a need but do so while expressly caring for the human component.

In short, businesses fueled not just by economic opportunity but also by empathy.

In 2016, the World Economic Forum (WEF) issued a paper titled *The Future of Jobs*. It cautioned that the acceleration, not just velocity, of technological change was on the brink of upsetting the economy incontrovertibly.[3]

The populist trends and election winners of 2016 bear out the paper's main premise. The rise of Donald Trump, Brexit in the UK, Populist parties winning elections across Europe from Austria to Italy: All capitalized on a fear of the future and a feeling of insecurity in the present.

The solution, at least prescribed by the WEF paper's authors, was to fill the sophisticated jobs of tomorrow with "reskilling and upskilling of today's workers."[4] Almost in lockstep, then-president Barack Obama announced a "computer science for all" program for elementary and high schools in the United States, which asked Congress for $4 billion. "[W]e have to make sure all our kids are equipped for the jobs of the future, which means not just being able to work with computers but developing the analytical and coding skills to power our innovation economy."[5]

That is *one* path forward. Some will go on to work in computing, science, technology, engineering, or mathematics. But let's not forget that for many of us, the rise of computers and online search engines doesn't draw us to this technical work—it *frees* us from it.

How many of us still do long division by paper rather than simply pulling out the calculators on our phones? How many of us study maps rather than leaning on GPS for directions? How many of us pick up an encyclopedia to answer a child's question rather than Google it?

My point: If the Industrial Revolution of the 1800s freed a large number of jobs from *physical* labor, the information revolution of the twenty-first century will free many jobs from *menial* labor. Baseline technical work will be left to the machines.

> Many jobs of the future won't compete with the technical capabilities and competence of computers; many jobs of the future will complement the capabilities and competence of computers.

Where does that leave us? Well, we find ourselves in a landscape where soft skills—communication, collaboration, critical thinking, creativity—will grow increasingly important and become equally valuable as hard skills. The emotional quotient—the ability to relate to others, understand emotional cues, and work together—will be seen as a vital counterpart to IQ.

This leaves us in a place where the *principles of hospitality*—the art of understanding people, caring for the details others don't, exercising empathy—stand to differentiate standout businesses and employees alike.

## The Increasing Need for the Meaning of Yes

Consider the traditional American shopping mall, not ironically, the place where I started my own career in real estate development after college. In retail, online giants like Amazon are increasingly dominating the market for everyday errands and purchases like groceries, hardware, and supplies. The malls I developed (traditional commercial strips) don't match the convenience and speed of ordering everything you need with the click of a computer mouse.

In spite of this fact, mall developers like Westfield (now owned by French real estate giant Unibail-Rodamco), Simon, and Caruso are all experiencing a veritable renaissance. They're creating places—and along the way, employment positions—bent on being destinations, not dead ends; customer-service leaders, not shopping-cart collectors. By focusing on creating experiences, they're taking the American mall from somewhere you *had* to go, to a place of community where you *want* to spend your time. These spaces are no longer just centers of transaction, but centers of *interaction*.

And you can't do that without people, or, in a more attenuated fine point, people who enjoy and derive meaning from taking care of others and creating experiences for them.

It's not just retail or customer service. It's the nurses who check on patient vitals and perform the critical task of making patients feel at ease. It's the police officers who don't just protect our towns and cities but are increasingly being tapped as liaisons from one neighborhood to another and as community builders when other social services fail. It's teachers, principals, and school administrators who are embracing personalized education, understanding that just because no two children learn the same doesn't mean one is inferior in ability or potential.

Let's be clear. This is not easy work. I should know—I've seen and experienced it firsthand.

My father, Sheldon, who recently passed, found himself in the throes of advanced Alzheimer's disease in his later years. There were days when he didn't know what week, month, or year it was, let alone where he was or who I was. But I considered myself lucky. I had the means to turn my home into an inpatient facility for him, so he had the medical care he needed, the comfort he deserved, and the patience, attention, and management that gave both him and me peace of mind.

When my father used to doze off or was content watching a movie, I had the opportunity to talk with his caretakers. I'd gotten to know their stories and even their families, and, in certain circumstances, had the opportunity to ask them about how they found themselves in their caretaker profession.

The one theme I heard most often, not just in relation to working with my father, but in past positions and assignments, is that the work can be grueling: early mornings, late nights, periods of waiting, mundane and repetitive questions. But the moments of connection can be more than just professionally rewarding; they can be nothing short of life-affirming and transcendent.

A nurse holding a baby in the NICU. A police officer de-escalating an altercation without force but through communication. A teacher helping a student learn a new concept, skill, or idea that the student hadn't been able to master before. A hospitality professional creating environments and experiences that put a traveler at ease. That's the work computers and technology will never be able to do. That's the work that we need now more than ever. And that's the work we need to show more appreciation for now than ever.

Earlier this year, I was crossing a walkway in Los Angeles when— boom!—out of seemingly nowhere, I found myself flung upward several feet into the air. A driver who hadn't been paying attention—we have reason to think he was texting—cruised through the intersection at approximately thirty-five miles per hour. He didn't stop when pedestrians, myself included, had the right of way. Luckily, I was the only one hit. No one else was hurt.

When I came to, I had a gash on my face over an inch long and ached from toe to torso. I'm tough, but admittedly, I was comforted by the legion of first responders who had already appeared on the scene. Next thing I knew, I was off to the hospital.

The following day and countless stitches later, I went to the local engine house to thank the firefighters who had taken care of me. At first, they were confused, even startled. Had I lost something? No, I assured them. I was here to thank them in person, to simply shake their hands.

"No one does this," they explained. "No one comes back the next day to say thank you."

My Saviors.

We all should be deeply startled by this reaction—one that I unfortunately expect is not limited to firefighters, Los Angeles, or this particular story. When it's so easy to send a text, shoot off an email, or simply not respond at all while hiding behind the shields of our technological devices, simple human-to-human shows of respect and recognition are even more valuable.

The simple truth is that as technology removes many of the informational barriers, real-world demand will only continue to grow for workers with empathy, social skills, and—dare I suggest it—an innate sense of hospitality, what the Meaning of Yes is all about.

This calls for a shift in perspective and strategy from employers and entrepreneurs.

As valuable as formal training in emotional skills might be, it's not at the heart of what makes people successful in emotional labor. The people I've worked with in hospitality at Diamond, in the medical initiatives and causes

I'm humbled to support in my own time, and the individuals who cared for my own father, all cite a "natural calling"—a gravitational force that pulled them to this line of work. No one yet has cited an academic course or lesson plan.

As I say this, I also caution all businesses and entrepreneurs from trying to *disingenuously* capitalize on their talents' social or emotional skills. What makes empathy and emotional skills in today's marketplace so valuable is the sheer fact that they *can't* be faked or forced—not sustainably or satisfactorily.

So what does all this mean? If computers, algorithms, and automation is making arduous cognitive work *less* of a day-to-day necessity for us (let's be honest, a computer computes better than a human) and makes arduous cognitive outputs *more* of a commodity we take for granted, then what *do* we value?

There's a twofold opportunity before us. We can choose to push efficiency to the brink, to focus narrowly on the idea of faster, leaner, more productive. But as that efficiency focus grows more pervasive, the stronger the demand, yearning, and, yes, need for genuine human connection becomes.

This book was my attempt to summarize influential and, if I did my job right, instructive moments from my life for the benefit of others. And my advice to any entrepreneur, intrapreneur, business professional, or student simply trying to figure things out is this: No matter what industry you're in, what path you go down, what career journey you choose, remember . . . We're all in hospitality.

> No matter what industry you're in, what path you go down, what career you choose, you get what you want by giving what others need.

This isn't necessarily a new conclusion, just a personal one. Consider how *New York Times* columnist Thomas Friedman ends his latest book, *Thank You for Being Late: An Optimist's Guide to Thriving in the Age of Accelerations*, which seeks to understand the "tectonic forces" shaping the world today:

I wasn't surprised that when I asked Surgeon General Murthy what was the biggest disease in America today, without hesitation he answered: "It's not cancer. It's not heart disease. *It's isolation.* It is the pronounced isolation that so many people are experiencing that is the great pathology of our lives today." How ironic. We are the most technologically connected generation in human history—and yet more people feel more isolated than ever. This only reinforces Murthy's earlier point—that the connections that matter most, and are in most short supply today, are the human-to-human ones.[6]

In the course of my career, I've seen technology-driven efficiency accomplish incredible things. It has brought people in developed countries astonishing quality and wealth to their standard of living, made possible and pervasive nearly instant access to information, and given small businesses and start-ups many of the same tools and resources as the Fortune 500. But I've also seen efficiency intensify the very real, in-demand need for true human connection, emotional skills, and an emphasis on hospitality.

The Meaning of Yes was my way of steeping empathy in the culture of Diamond Resorts. As much as it was an opportunity for me, for emerging businesses it will be an imperative.

## ACKNOWLEDGMENTS

'd be remiss in releasing my first book without a full-hearted recognition that this work—and moreover, all the stories contained within it—wouldn't have been possible without the love, support, and, yes, at times good-natured tolerance of my incredible family.

I want you to know that I don't always do things the right way, but you inspire me to always try to do the right thing. For that, I'm grateful.

To my eldest son, Kevin, who never stops astounding me. You have your mom's imaginative instincts combined with your own sense of style, spunk, and sophistication. (If you ended up watching the second *Undercover Boss* episode I was featured in, the much-improved costume—spiky bleached hair, goggle-size glasses, and, yes, actual pierced ears—was his idea.) Kevin, your creativity, positivity, and dedication will take you far in life. I count my blessings in being able to watch you grow.

To my Jacob, who is currently enrolled at the Dodge College of Film and Media Arts at Chapman University (while simultaneously pursuing entrepreneurial endeavors of his own, might I add). There's a passion you bring to your pursuits—from your studies in film to the energy you share with friends and family—that's uniquely you. Never lose it. Your hard work and zeal for life goes unmatched. And so, as you set out to become Hollywood's next great creative producer, suffice it to say that I can't wait to see you take the world by storm, on your terms.

To Jaden, my Renaissance Man—as you officially start your college career at the University of Pennsylvania, all I can say is watch out, East Coast! You're an old soul, but more importantly, a truly *kind* soul. I smile every time I see you set a new goal for yourself, and then—rather than simply reaching it—end up far, *far* exceeding it. Set your sights high, Jaden—they simply don't make them like you anymore. I hope you know you make your dad very, very proud.

To Tatiana, my youngest and only daughter. You have a love for singing that I know will sustain you through a performer's career of highs and lows. Tati, there's no one that makes me laugh quite like you, no one that makes my heart swell quite like you, no one who makes me want to make the world a better place, quite like you. You're smart as a whip, crazy talented, and wonderfully compassionate. Never stop using your voice, not just for singing, but also for the causes you care about. My daughter, mark my words, one day we'll be seeing your name in lights.

Kids, if there's one thing your mom and I hope to teach you, it's that the world is what you make of it. So go out there and make your dreams come true. You've already made ours.

And to my parents. Dad, you were tough on me. You pushed me. You challenged me. God knows, we had our disagreements. But we made one hell of a team. Mom, thank you for being there for me. Let me quite simply and insufficiently say, I love you.

# NOTES

## INTRODUCTION

1   Jennifer Wang, "Timeshare Resort Company Founder, Undercover Boss, Is Big Winner in Apollo's Latest Deal," *Forbes,* July 2, 2016, https://www.forbes.com/sites/jenniferwang/2016/07/02/timeshare-resort-company-founder-undercover-boss-is-big-winner-in-apollos-latest-deal/#1c15d7e7069c.

2   Stephen Cloobeck, "The Trump Tourism Slump," *U.S. News & World Report*, April 28, 2017, https://www.usnews.com/opinion/economic-intelligence/articles/2017-04-28/how-donald-trump-hurts-international-tourism-and-the-us-economy.

3   Patrick Seitz, "Apple Within Spitting Distance of $1 Trillion Market Cap," *Investor's Business Daily*, May 4, 2018, https://www.investors.

com/news/technology/click/apple-1-trillion-market-cap/; Paul R. La Monica, "Apple Inches Closer to $1 Trillion Market Value," CNN Money, May 7, 2018, http://money.cnn.com/2018/05/07/investing/apple-trillion-dollar-market-value/index.html.

4    "What Is Apple's Current Mission Statement and How Does It Differ from Steve Jobs' Original Ideals?" Investopedia, last modified January 8, 2018, https://www.investopedia.com/ask/answers/042315/what-apples-current-mission-statement-and-how-does-it-differ-steve-jobs-original-ideals.asp. Note that Apple's original mission statement differs from the product-centric version it has adopted today: "Apple designs Macs, the best personal computers in the world, along with OS X, iLife, iWork and professional software. Apple leads the digital music revolution with its iPods and iTunes online store. Apple has reinvented the mobile phone with its revolutionary iPhone and App store, and is defining the future of mobile media and computing devices with iPad."

5    "Our Company," Google, accessed January 23, 2018, https://www.google.com/intl/en/about/our-company/.

6    "About," Microsoft, accessed January 23, 2018, https://www.microsoft.com/en-us/about/default.aspx.

7    Barbara Farfan, "Amazon.com's Mission Statement," The Balance, last modified December 24, 2017, https://www.thebalance.com/amazon-mission-statement-4068548.

8    "FAQs," Facebook Investor Relations, accessed January 23, 2018, https://investor.fb.com/resources/default.aspx.

9    "Travel, Tourism, and Hospitality Spotlight," SelectUSA, accessed January 23, 2018, https://www.selectusa.gov/travel-tourism-and-hospitality-industry-united-states.

## CHAPTER 1: BEGINNINGS

1  Peter A. Coclanis, "Business of Chicago," *Encyclopedia of Chicago*, accessed February 13, 2017, http://www.encyclopedia.chicagohistory. org/pages/198.html.

## CHAPTER 2: STRIKING OUT ON MY OWN

1  Hapimag, "About Us, History," accessed May 11, 2018, https://www. hapimag.com/en/what/about-us/history.html.

2  "A (Very) Brief History of the Timeshare Industry," Inside the Gate, accessed June 29, 2017, http://www.insidethegate.com/ about-timeshare/history/.

## CHAPTER 3: THE SUNTERRA SAGA

1  Todd Pack, "Sunterra Seeking $150 million in Damages from Andersen; Blames Failure on Accounting Firm," Hotel Online, accessed February 20, 2018, http://www.hotel-online.com/News/ PR2002_2nd/Jun02_Sunterra.html.

2  Securities and Exchange Commission, *Schedule 13D: Sunterra Corporation,* June 23, 2006, https://www.sec.gov/Archives/edgar/ data/1016577/000114036106009598/sc13d.htm.

3  Ibid.

4  Hubble Smith, "Shareholder Calls for Sale of Sunterra," *Las Vegas Review-Journal,* July 1, 2006.

5  "Sunterra Fires Its Own CEO," *Pacific Business News,* July 27, 2006, http://www.bizjournals.com/pacific/stories/2006/07/24/daily35. html.

6   James Weissenborn (former interim CEO to Sunterra; founding and managing partner, Mackinac Partners), in discussion with the author, March 2017.

7   Christopher Boyd, "Sunterra Hit by Lawsuits as It Restructures," *Orlando Sentinel*, September 21, 2006, http://articles.orlandosentinel.com/2006-09-21/business/ SUNTERRA21_1_sunterra-financial-operations-financial-results.

## CHAPTER 4: TOWARD A TURNAROUND

1   Lynda Resnick, *Rubies in the Orchard: How to Uncover the Hidden Gems in Your Business*, with Francis Wilkinson (New York: Doubleday, 2009).

2   "Diamond Resorts Buying Sunterra for 700m," *Orlando Business Journal*, March 12, 2007 https://www.bizjournals.com/orlando/ stories/2007/03/12/daily7.html.

## CHAPTER 5: THE MEANING OF YES

1   Brian de Haaff, "The Obsession Amazon CEO Jeff Bezos Avoids (and So Should You)," Inc., July 25, 2017, https://www.inc.com/brian-de- haaff/brilliant-ceos-do-not-obsess-over-competitors-n.html.

## CHAPTER 6: BE MY GUEST

1   For those of you who are politically inclined, let me share in the spirit of full disclosure that Frank Luntz has been a longtime Republican strategist, while I myself have been a lifelong supporter of the Democratic party in my home state of Nevada and beyond.

Frank and I have our differences of opinion, but I've always enjoyed our conversations for their richness of debate, open-mindedness, and underlying respect. We need more cross-party conversation and collaboration in this country, not less.

## CHAPTER 7: FROM A CULTURE OF NO TO THE MEANING OF YES

1   Ashley Lutz, "Nordstrom's Employee Handbook Has Only One Rule," *Business Insider,* October 13, 2014, http://www.businessinsider.com/nordstroms-employee-handbook-2014-10?IR=T.

2   Joshua Freed, "Q&A: CEO Discusses Delta's Revival, Flying Today," *USA TODAY,* June 27, 2013, https://www.usatoday.com/story/todayinthesky/2013/06/27/qa-ceo-discusses-deltas-revival-flying-today/2462875/.

## CHAPTER 8: EMPOWER THE PERIPHERY

1   Anahad O'Connor, "The Claim: Heart Attacks Are More Common on Mondays," *New York Times*, March 14, 2006, http://www.nytimes.com/2006/03/14/health/14real.html.

2   Passover Haggadah, deluxe ed. (n.p.: General Foods Corporation, 1965).

3   Exodus 22:21 (NASB).

4   Exodus 2:22 (KJV).

5   Matthew 25:35 (NASB).

6   Hebrews 13:2 (NASB).

7   Atithi Devo Bhava (Taittiriya Upanishad, Shikshavalli, I.20).

8    An-Nisa 4:36.


## CHAPTER 9: EMBRACING A COLLABORATIVE MERITOCRACY

1    Attributed to the notable American oncologist Howard Skipper, whose
     work in cancer research, science, and modeling has paved the way for
     today's most modern and successful treatments.


## CHAPTER 10: MY BUSINESS CARD ON EVERY FRONT DESK

1    Bill Dann, "The Power of Accountability," Professional
     Growth Systems, accessed on February 18, 2018, http://www.
     professionalgrowthsystems.com/growthlines/power-accountability/.


## CHAPTER 11: TAKING THE LONG VIEW

1    "Case Study: The Collapse of Lehman Brothers," Investopedia, last
     modified December 11, 2017, http://www.investopedia.com/articles/
     economics/09/lehman-brothers-collapse.asp#ixzz4f1251C5z.

2    J. R. Brent Ritchie, Carlos Mario Amaya Molinar, Douglas C.
     Fretchling, "Impacts of the World Recession and Economic Crisis on
     Tourism: North America," *Journal of Travel Research* 49, no. 1 (2010):
     5–15, doi:10.1177/0047287509353193.

3    John de Graaf, "Let's Make More Vacation Time a National
     Priority," Diamond Resorts International, November 10, 2015,
     https://www.diamondresorts.com/smart-travel-tips/view/
     lets-make-more-vacation-time-national-priority.

4    "Health Benefits of Vacations," Health Net, accessed June 29, 2017,

https://www.healthnet.com/portal/home/content/iwc/home/articles/
health_benefits_of_vacations.action.

5   Beth Howard, "5 Scientific Reasons You Should Go On
Vacation," Oprah.com, accessed February 18, 2018, https://
www.huffingtonpost.com/entry/vacation-health-benefits_
us_573e3000e4b0613b5129c2df?utm_hp_ref=own-happier.

6   "EY at a Glance," EY.com, accessed February 18, 2018, http://www.
ey.com/us/en/newsroom/facts-and-figures.

7   Alina Tugend, "Take a Vacation, for Your Health's Sake," *New York
Times,* June 8, 2008, http://www.nytimes.com/2008/06/08/business/
worldbusiness/08iht-07shortcuts.13547623.html.

8   de Graaf, "More Vacation Time."

9   Dan Ring, "CEO James Murren Turned Around MGM Resorts and
Now Wants to Reverse the Fortunes of Springfield," *MassLive,* April 22,
2013, http://www.masslive.com/news/index.ssf/2013/04/ceo_james_
murren_turned_around.html.

10  Alana Horowitz, "15 People Who Were Fired
before They Became Filthy Rich," *Business Insider,*
April 25, 2011, http://www.businessinsider.
com/15-people-who-were-fired-before-they-became-filthy-rich-2011-4.

11  Ibid.

12  J. K. Rowling, "The Fringe Benefits of Failure, and the Importance
of Imagination," transcript and YouTube video, 24:12, Harvard
University, https://news.harvard.edu/gazette/story/2008/06/
text-of-j-k-rowling-speech/.

## CHAPTER 12: ONCE AN ENTREPRENEUR, ALWAYS AN INTRAPRENEUR

1   Julie Zeveloff, "The Incredible Life of Steve Wynn: How a Small-Time
    Bingo Operator Became One of the World's Biggest Hotel Moguls,"
    *Business Insider*, July 11, 2011, http://www.businessinsider.com/
    steve-wynn-las-vegas-biography-2011-7#.

## CHAPTER 14: SEEKING INSPIRATION FROM ALL PLACES

1   "Bloomberg TV Exclusive with Georgia's Saakashvili This
    Weekend," Embassy of Georgia to the United States of
    America, August 31, 2007, http://usa.mfa.gov.ge/index.
    php?lang_id=ENG&sec_id=595&info_id=192.

2   "Economy Rankings," The World Bank, June 2017, http://www.
    doingbusiness.org/rankings.

## CHAPTER 17: GROWING THE PIE

1   "Las Vegas," History.com, accessed June 29, 2017, http://www.history.
    com/topics/las-vegas.

2   Ibid.

3   Bob Shemeligian, "Strip Project Spruces Up Main Thoroughfare," *Las
    Vegas Sun*, March 22, 1996, https://lasvegassun.com/news/1996/
    mar/22/strip-project-spruces-up-main-thoroughfare/.

4   "Las Vegas Strip Scenic Byway," Travel Nevada, accessed
    February 18, 2018, https://travelnevada.com/discover/26273/
    las-vegas-strip-scenic-byway.

5   Las Vegas Convention and Visitors Authority, *Historical Las Vegas*

*Visitor Statistics,* February 2017, http://www.lvcva.com/includes/
content/images/media/docs/Historical-1970-to-2016.pdf.


## CHAPTER 18: BRAND USA

1    U.S. Travel Association and Oxford Economics, *The Lost Decade,*
February 2010, https://www.ustravel.org/research/lost-decade.

2    Mary Ann McNulty, "Feds, USTA Plan Travel Promotion Act
Implementation," *Business Travel News,* March 3, 2010, http://www.
businesstravelnews.com/Business-Globalization/Feds-USTA-Plan-
Travel-Promotion-Act-Implementation. There's no doubt that the
shock and terror of the September 11, 2001, attacks cast a long shadow
on the American tourism industry. But a 9 percent drop over ten years,
against a context of growth, can't be totally explained by one event,
however abhorrent.

3    "The Lost Decade: The High Costs of America's Failure to Compete for
International Travel," U.S. Travel Association Report, February 2010,
https://www.ustravel.org/research/lost-decade.

4    Jessica Zuckerman, "Travel Promotion: Brand USA Marked by Waste
and Abuse," The Heritage Foundation, October 10, 2012, http://www.
heritage.org/immigration/report/travel-promotion-brand-usa-marked-
waste-and-abuse.

5    Marnie Hunter, "U.S. Travel Promotion Bill Signed into Law," *CNN,*
March 4, 2010, http://www.cnn.com/2010/TRAVEL/03/04/travel.
promotion.act/index.html.

6    Michelle Baran, "Marketing by Brand USA Produces an
ROI of 47:1," *Travel Weekly,* February 17, 2014, http://
www.travelweekly.com/Travel-News/Government/
Marketing-by-Brand-USA-produces-an-ROI-of-47-to-1.

7   Ibid.


## CHAPTER 19: WE'RE ALL IN HOSPITALITY NOW

1   John Mackey and Raj Sisodia, *Conscious Capitalism: Liberating the Heroic Spirit of Business* (Boston: Harvard Business School Publishing, 2014), 12–16.

2   Michael Milken, "Prosperity and Social Capital," *The Wall Street Journal*, June 23, 1999.

3   World Economic Forum, *The Future of Jobs*, January 2016, http://www3.weforum.org/docs/WEF_Future_of_Jobs.pdf.

4   Ibid, v.

5   Ahiza Garcia, "Obama on the 'Jobs of the Future,'" BRProud, accessed June 29, 2017, http://www.brproud.com/news/obama-on-the-jobs-of-the-future/352181493.

6   Thomas Friedman, *Thank You for Being Late: An Optimist's Guide to Thriving in the Age of Accelerations* (New York: Farrar, Straus and Giroux, 2016), 490–491.

financial crisis of 2008. *See* Great
Recession
financial technology, 224–225
Flaskey, Mike, 115–116, 120
free-market economics, 195, 222
Friedman, Thomas, 232–233
future
business opportunities of, 18,
222–223, 227–233
planning IT for, 193
*Future of Jobs, The* (WEF), 227

**G**

Georgia, 166–174
good, doing well by doing, 9–10,
129–135
Grant, Adam, 16–17
Gray, Paul, 33
Great Recession, 129–139
grit, role in success, 139–143
guests. *See* customers; hospitality;
Meaning of Yes philosophy;
*specific principles of hospitality*

**H**

Hapimag (Hotel- und Apartmen-
thaus Immobilien Anlage AG),
32
Hinduism, hospitality in, 104
Hinton, Dale, 169
Holzman, Eli, 181, 185, 187
hospitality. *See also* Diamond
Resorts International; Meaning of Yes philosophy; *specific
principles of hospitality*

Brand USA focus on, 212–215
as calling, 104–106
caring for details in, 74–75
focus on, role in success, 3–6
and future of business, 227–233
in Georgia, 169–174
improving with technology,
192–193
as involving every industry,
221–227, 232–233, xii–xiii
principles of, 6–10, 17–18
in religious traditions, 104
seeking inspiration from all
places, 165–178
universality of, 173–174
hospitality industry, 1–2, 6, 22–24,
131–132. *See also specific
companies*
Hughes, Howard, 197
human capital, 224–225, ix–xii. *See
also* employees
Hyatt Corporation, 33

**I**

improvement, continuous, 7–8,
89–95, 148–153, 162, 164
Independent Development Corporation, 35–36
Innisfree Corporations, 33
inspiration, seeking from all places,
152–153, 165–178
institutionalized intrapreneurship,
162–164, 187–188
international travel to US, 202–
205. *See also* Brand USA

S tephen J. Cloobeck is a self-made entrepreneur with more than thirty years' experience across every aspect of hospitality design, development, and deployment.

As the original founder and former CEO and chairman of Diamond Resorts International (NYSE:DRII)—a business that grew to become the second-largest vacation-ownership company worldwide with more than four hundred properties across thirty-three countries in its portfolio—Cloobeck made a name for himself as the industry's most adamant advocate for radical customer service, what he calls embracing the Meaning of Yes.

For his commitment to serving the hospitality industry and amplifying its economic impact nationwide, Cloobeck was appointed by Commerce Secretary Gary Locke to serve as the inaugural chairman of the board on Brand USA Inc., a US government–formed nonprofit corporation with the sole mission of promoting travel to the United States. As Brand USA's leading voice, Cloobeck coordinated with the Department of Homeland

Security, the Department of State, the Department of Commerce, Congress, the White House, and leading American businesses in a first-ever effort to efficiently, effectively, and economically make the United States a more welcoming and accessible international travel destination for millions of would-be visitors around the globe.

But to Cloobeck's own amusement, he is perhaps most frequently recognized for his appearances on CBS's hit TV show *Undercover Boss.* Featured on multiple episodes across multiple seasons, Cloobeck to this day ranks as the "most generous boss" that's ever participated in the unscripted program.

Cloobeck works with many charities and civic organizations, including but not limited to: the Prostate Cancer Foundation, FasterCures, Keep Memory Alive, Water.org, the Brent Shapiro Foundation for Drug Prevention, and various educational initiatives. In personal efforts to assist Diamond Resorts team members dealing with unexpected life events, Cloobeck founded the Diamond Resorts International Team Member Crisis Fund (now the Diamond Resorts International Foundation) in 2012, an unprecedented initiative that continues to offer aid to Diamond staff worldwide struggling with personal difficulties.

Cloobeck received a degree in psychology from Brandeis University in 1983 by the seat of his pants, only to learn after graduation that he had been grappling with undiagnosed dyslexia all that time.

Cloobeck will be donating all of this book's author proceeds to dyslexia research, education, and supportive causes.